WHAT THE PRESS IS SAYING. . .

"A superb job of creating order out of chaos."

— *Mass. Lawyers Weekly*

"Easy to read...explains clearly some of Medicaid's most complex inscrutabilities."

— *Library Journal*

"Simply written and well-designed ... to help make Medicaid planning options approachable by the nonprofessional reader."

— *United Retirement Bulletin*

"Stripped of the frills, the message [is] pretty simple: If you plan, you and your family can hold on to your money; if you don't, it could all go to pay for a nursing home."

— *The Boston Globe*

"Gordon has become something of a guru to the elderly...He is the guy...who tells them how to avoid turning their golden years into a nightmare."

— *Daily Item*

HOW TO PROTECT YOUR LIFE SAVINGS

from Catastrophic Illness and Nursing Homes

A Handbook for Financial Survival

**By Harley Gordon
with Jane Daniel**

© Copyright 1990 by
Harley Gordon and Jane Daniel

First Edition Published 1990
Second Printing

Designed by Daniel & Daniel
       Ronald Duce
       Suzanne Lucien
       John Perry

Printed in the United States of America

Library of Congress Catalog Card Number 90-80119

ISBN   0-9625667-0-5

FINANCIAL PLANNING INSTITUTE, INC.
P.O. Box 135
Boston, MA 02258
(617) 244-2216

Author's Note

What will this book give you?

Knowledge.
Knowledge equals power.
And power equals CONTROL.

We all struggle to keep control over our lives and our assets. Knowledge is the key to control. We learn how to invest, how to save and when to change course. We struggle to maintain our balance.

If you are facing a catastrophic illness, you are beginning to realize what a loss of control can do to your life. Loss of control over your assets is usually not far behind. Lack of knowledge about how to protect life savings exposes you to financial ruin.

Most self-help books encourage you to do-it-yourself. In this area, it's not a good idea. My assumption is that you *will* need professional help.

It is not the intention of this book to encourage you to hide all your assets and claim poverty. You have a responsibility to pay your fair share. It is my intent to help you protect the balance of your assets and, in particular, your house.

In lecturing to audiences of both professional and senior citizens' groups, I have seen that they have one thing in common—everyone's confused. Some people know they are in the dark. Some people think they have the answer. Few do.

This manual is written to clear up the confusion. It tells you in simple language not just what the problem is but what you can do about it. It explains the laws, but there isn't a word of "legalese" on these pages.

The solutions to problems offered here are not textbook answers, because there are no textbooks on this subject. Instead, I have drawn upon my experiences and those of other professionals whom I trust to give you a street-wise understanding of a complex and sometimes bizarre system.

After reading this book you can make your decisions, however painful and difficult they may be, with confidence that you are acting in an informed and responsible manner.

Harley Gordon

Whose Problem Is This, Anyway?

Facing up to long term care

We are hearing a lot about nursing homes and their cost these days. We hear that nursing homes are expensive. We hear that old people are going into nursing homes and that the taxpayers have to pick up the cost. With the current squeeze on state and federal budgets, people are getting upset at what appears to be yet another drain on the taxpayers' dollars.

What's really happening?

The answer is that we are facing a period of tremendous social change. As we near the end of the century, a national crisis is being played out in average homes, of average families, all across America.
You are contributing to the crisis if you watch your cholesterol, exercise, take your vitamins, and see your doctor regularly, because you are probably going to live longer. In fact, more and more people are living longer. In the next 40 years, the population of people over 65 will almost double. Today, the fastest growing segment of the population is people 85 and older.

That's what's causing the crisis. With increasing age comes more frailty and illness. On an individual level, families all over the country are coming face to face with sweeping social change as they struggle to take care of the aging members of their families.

When their elders fall victim to a catastrophic illness like a stroke or Alzheimer's disease, families try to take care of them as best and as long as they can. To do it, family members often give up their normal way of life and their peace of mind. Marriages are stressed to the breaking point; children live with constant tension. Taking care of a chronically ill person at home makes the whole family chronically ill.

The idea that selfish people are dumping their relatives in nursing homes is pure myth. In fact, 85 percent of the frail elderly are cared for at home. Of the remaining 15 percent, half have no immediate family and the rest usually have relatives who are themselves frail and elderly.

The problem of coping with a serious illness can be so painful that people who haven't experienced it can hardly imagine it. Every year, a million families struggle against heartbreak and exhaustion and finally give up. In the end they make what many call the most painful decision of their lives: they put a beloved spouse or parent in a nursing home.

But the tragedy doesn't end there. Medicare and private insurance do not cover the cost of long-term care. When one spouse is admitted to a nursing home, in only 13 weeks, on average, the couple's entire life savings are wiped out.

Then, when their savings are gone, Medicaid, a program for poor people who have no other means to pay, steps in to pick up the nursing home cost. The state determines how much money the well spouse is allowed to keep. For people of modest means, the well spouse will be impoverished and may live out the remainder of his or her life perilously close to, or below, the poverty line.

For both spouses, the sick and the well, control over their money is gone, and with it goes the dignity, security and independence they worked all their lives to attain. It's terrifying. As one elderly woman put it, "I wake up every morning in fear."

This does not have to happen. In fact, social policy recognizes that impoverishment is a bad thing. Therefore, the law allows us to avoid financial ruin. There are a number of strategies to do this, like putting assets in trusts or giving them away, but until recently, few people knew about them.

When assets are protected this way, there is no safety net, in the form of private insurance or public entitlement programs, to bridge the gap. Should a catastrophic illness strike, Medicaid, a form of welfare, is all that's left to pick up the cost.

And that makes many taxpayers furious. Their argument goes, "I don't want my tax dollars to pay for your mother's nursing home bill." In short, "It's your problem; you handle it."

Given the seriousness of the threat, people need to have a way to protect themselves. Unfortunately, there's almost nothing that responsible people can do, other than to use whatever legal means are available to protect (some would say "hide") their assets.

Private insurance is not the answer for people of modest means because nursing home policies are too expensive.

A disturbing number of these policies are riddled with restrictions, exceptions, and deliberate fuzzy language that disqualifies the policy-holder from ever collecting much of anything.

Another insurance trap is that most policies provide insufficient or no defense against the erosion of benefits by the rising cost of health care. If you buy a nursing home policy today and are institutionalized in ten years, it is unlikely that you will have enough benefits to cover more than a small fraction of your nursing home bill.

Many states have adopted regulations to try to eliminate the worst abuses, but senior citizens' groups feel that the effort hasn't gone nearly far enough.

In addition to these drawbacks, the policies are too expensive for the vast majority of seniors. Of all older Americans between the ages of 65 and 79, a whopping 84 percent cannot afford to pay the average cost of basic nursing home insurance policies from nine leading companies, according to one recent study.

So what some people are doing is protecting themselves as best they can by using the provisions available under the law. Are these people "flimflamming Medicaid" by taking advantage of loopholes to dump their relatives onto the taxpayers backs? Are they welfare free-loaders, "false poor" riding a "gravy train," as one national magazine asserts?

Here's a typical story:

My father died from a hereditary disorder that caused a long, slow degeneration of his mind and body. I helped my mother care for him till he mercifully suffered a fatal stroke. I'm convinced that the enormous effort contributed to my mother's death a year after his.

Now I am at risk for the disease. I am 16 years older than my wife. I have two children and a disabled brother who depends upon us for assistance, financial and otherwise.

My wife inherited a house from her mother. We both work full-time and try to save money for our old age. With two children and my brother, it isn't easy to put money aside. I worry constantly about how my family will manage if I develop the disease. I have to do everything I can, now, to protect them if something happens to me.

This case is the norm, not the exception. Sure, there are probably a few wealthy people with high-priced lawyers and accountants who are getting their relatives on Medicaid. True, Medicaid was designed to provide for the poor who have no other means to pay for long term care. But that's the point — there is no system there for the middle class. Does that mean that it makes sense to drive millions of elderly Americans into poverty before we lend them a hand?

Most people accept responsibility for dealing with misfortunes that befall them, even those which occur through no fault of their own. Most people are willing to pay their fair share.

But what is a fair share? What does society owe to the millions of hard-working senior citizens whose taxes have carried this country's economy for half a century? There is no blame or culpability here. Catastrophic illness is an act of God. People do not choose to become critically ill.

When they have outlived their good health and independence, should society say, "Hey, it's your problem; you handle it?"

This issue is a one of the biggest challenges we face as we move toward the next century. It is an individual problem; it is a social problem: Where does responsibility lie? We are being called upon to examine our fundamental beliefs about ourselves and our society.

We operate on the basic assumption that it is the individual's responsibility to society to work for the greatest good for the greatest number. That's why we obey the laws and pay our taxes.

Conversely, it is society's responsibility to the individual to do the same. The whole, in its magnitude, promotes the well-being of the individual. That's why, when an earthquake or a hurricane or another act of God strikes, our collective taxes and insurance reserves pay for disaster relief. But when catastrophic illness strikes, there is no adequate "disaster relief."

Senior citizens have held up their end of the bargain. We as a society are not holding up ours.

The problem, in the proportions we are witnessing today, is new. Government and private industry have not yet come up with the answers. Until they do, individuals must use whatever legal means are available to protect themselves.

TABLE OF CONTENTS

4

HOW TO PROTECT ASSETS WHEN THERE'S TIME TO PLAN

5

WHAT TO DO WHEN YOU DON'T HAVE TIME TO PROTECT YOUR ASSETS

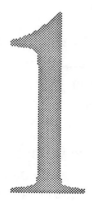

THE PROBLEM

THE PROBLEM

At the turn of the century, the average life expectancy in the United States was 47 years. As we reach the last decade of this century, life expectancy has increased to 75 years and people commonly live much longer. The fastest growing segment of our society is the population over 65.

The longer we live, the more we become susceptible to frailties and illnesses that may incapacitate rather than kill us. As a society and as individuals we are facing some fundamental questions in our struggle to care for an expanding older population.

One of the major problems is: Who takes care of us when we can't manage on our own anymore? Who takes care of our parents? Who takes care of people who are so incapacitated that they need long-term custodial attention?

More and more, the answer is a nursing home. Nursing homes provide long-term custodial care for conditions or illnesses that incapacitate a person—Alzheimer's and related senile dementia, Parkinson's disease, crippling rheumatoid arthritis, stroke, and other major disabilities.

If you are over 65, you may become the one out of every six people confined to a nursing home for some period of time. Over the age of 80, your chances are fifty-fifty.

Those are sobering statistics.

The costs are just as disturbing. In the northeast, the cost of a nursing home bed can run up to $60,000 a year. Although the cost may be less in other parts of the country, income and savings are proportionately less as well. Few people can afford those kinds of expenses out of pocket.

Ultimately the question arises: Who pays for long-term nursing home care? As we will see, there are few sources available.

The Harsh Realities

When a serious illness strikes a family member, relatives go into emotional shock. The last thing they think about is the financial aspects of long-term disability. It may seem distasteful, insensitive, or even crass to talk about money with someone who has just been diagnosed as having a long-term debilitating and possibly fatal disease.

Spouses are emotionally devastated by the thought that their life partner will one day be incapacitated and need a nursing home. Family members may have as much difficulty talking with the well spouse as with the person who is ill. Even though some members of the family may realize that a good, honest discussion is in order, it's one thing to know it and quite another to do it.

The problem of talking about finances and making plans is particularly difficult when it is the husband who has been stricken. Most elderly couples have enjoyed traditional marriages in which the wife's role was one of dutiful homemaker and the husband's one of active provider. Though their roles are equally important, one of the consequences of this arrangement is that the wife has generally had little or no experience in managing assets or taking care of finances. The worst time for her to learn about money is when she hears that her spouse has a debilitating illness that will ultimately put him in a nursing home.

This situation, combined with a strong denial instinct in the face of pain, postpones the time when the couple seeks or accepts help in finding ways to protect themselves financially. Inaction can mean that a lifetime of accumulated assets is wiped out because of an illness over which no one has any control.

Heartbreaking Stories, Painful Decisions

Mr. A. was diagnosed as having Parkinson's disease. Mr. and Mrs. A.'s daughter Gloria tried to talk with her mother about her dad's worsening condition and what plans they should be making for the time when she and her mother could no longer care for him at home. Gloria tried to find times when her mother seemed open to discussing the topic. But whenever the subject was raised, Mrs. A. became agitated and walked out of the room.

Mrs. A. could not face the probability that her husband's illness would one day require nursing home care. The nature of the illness itself supported that denial because of its slow onset and insidious development. Despite the fact that the symptoms were becoming more pronounced, the mother failed to see what the daughter could see all too clearly. Gloria knew that her father was getting worse and that her mother was withdrawing, unable to make any decisions, unsure of what to do next.

Open communication is difficult under the stress of a serious illness but it is essential to planning for long-term care. And when the relationship between one or both parents and their offspring was never particularly close, the difficulties are compounded. Over the years personality clashes develop and disappointments set in on both sides.

Communication problems usually have nothing to do with the love that the parents and children feel for each other. But because of these difficulties, when the diagnosis of a catastrophic illness is made, the children may not even be informed. The offspring may go along for months sensing something is wrong with their mother or father and not knowing what to do about it. One of the toughest discussions a person can ever have with a parent starts with the question, "What's wrong?"

Robert L. had suspected for a year that his father had Alzheimer's. Robert had never had a warm relationship with his father and ever since his mother's death they had drifted apart. Because of their lack of closeness, Robert was unable to talk with his father about his concern over the old man's health and his father was unable to ask his son for help. Together they were both victims. Robert felt anguish over his father's worsening condition. His pain was complicated by the worry that, as an only child, he would have to be the one to put his dad in a nursing home and find a way to pay for it.

Another difficult situation sometimes occurs where unmarried siblings are involved. Elderly people who have chosen not to marry tend to be self-reliant. What family ties they have are usually to brothers and sisters. (It's surprising how many of these people never married because they chose instead to take care of an aging parent.) While the siblings may be independent, it is not uncommon for them to hold their assets together. And although they are close, that doesn't mean that they plan together or tell each other everything.

Dolores and Edna were sisters who lived around the corner from each other. One night, at 2:00 am, Edna was awakened by a call from the police. An officer had found Dolores wandering down the middle of the street in her nightgown. As close as they were, her sister never confided to her what Edna had suspected for many months: Dolores was losing her faculties. Edna knew she had to get help for her sister because Dolores was putting herself in danger. But what would it cost and how would the bills be paid? All their money was held jointly, so what affected Dolores also affected Edna.

Sometimes a situation is thrust upon a family member who never expected it. When an unmarried or widowed elderly person survives his or her siblings, who makes the arrangements for care when they need it? Often it is a favorite niece or nephew, the one they treated as one of their own. Nephews and nieces are usually completely in the dark about the older generation's financial affairs. What they know is generally limited to what they learned at Thanksgiving and Christmas celebrations.

William knew for years that his Aunt Claire suffered from chronic depression. Somehow she always took care of herself so the problem was never addressed. Aunt Claire never acknowledged that there was anything wrong. One day, William received a phone call from her doctor (she'd given his name as next of kin): "Would you be willing to be your aunt's guardian?" he was asked. He wasn't too surprised that she was failing. What bothered him was that he had no idea how to face or help her, and what resources were available to provide for her care in a nursing home if it became necessary.

The previous illustrations show the various and difficult ways that people come face to face with the problem of catastrophic illness. Facing the facts of the situation as quickly as possible is of major importance because *the options are limited and timing is crucial.* The alternative to dealing effectively with the financial implications of a major illness is devastation for the family both monetarily and emotionally.

People work and struggle a lifetime to set aside enough to provide security for themselves and their offspring. The first step in dealing with the problem of protecting assets from chronic illness and long-term nursing home care is to learn about it. Knowledge is the best preparation for confronting the problem head on.

We will look at ways to protect assets in two scenarios:

First: When there is time to plan because the illness has been diagnosed early and progresses slowly.

Second: When there is a crisis, such as a stroke or an accident that requires long-term care immediately.

ALTERNATIVES TO NURSING HOMES?

ALTERNATIVES TO NURSING HOMES?

Contrary to popular belief, nursing homes are not places that families choose as their first option; they are a last resort. Families will struggle for years to keep their parents or relatives out of a nursing home.

With the exception of a stroke or an accident, most conditions that incapacitate people start slowly and run their downhill course over a period of years. At the beginning, it is easy for a family to overlook the financial impact of providing care at some future date when the sick person's health has deteriorated. Family members tend to hope that they will somehow be able to manage at home.

Unfortunately, best intentions notwithstanding, people underestimate the physical, emotional, and logistical burdens created by trying to cope with a person who is seriously ill. If they do recognize these problems, the family often assumes that a hospital will be a resource when the time comes that they cannot handle the burdens.

That is no longer the case. Here's why:

Hospitals — Not Anymore!

Hospitals have historically been paid through one of four sources:

- Cash
- Medicare
- Medicaid
- Private insurance (such as HMOs and Blue Cross/ Blue Shield)

Cash A hospital stay in most metropolitan areas can cost up to $1,000 or more a day depending upon type of care.

Medicare Medicare should not be confused with Medicaid. Medicare is the primary insurance plan that covers people on Social Security. It pays for hospital and medical expenses. The vast majority of older people in hospitals are covered by Medicare.

Prior to 1984, Medicare paid whatever bills were submitted by the hospital for a person's care. The expense to the federal government was so enormous that in 1984 the system was drastically reformed. The federal government established a reimbursement system called Diagnostic Related Groupings (DRGs). Under this system, Medicare pays the hospital a flat rate for a person's illness. If the hospital can stabilize the patient for a cost that is less than what Medicare pays, they keep the change. On the other hand, if the patient cannot be stabilized for the designated amount, the hospital usually pays the additional costs out of pocket. Therefore, there is a strong economic incentive for a hospital to move a patient out as soon as he is stabilized.

As a result the word "stabilized" has a much different meaning today than it did prior to 1984. In the old days, a person could stay in the hospital almost indefinitely, until he either got significantly better or died. Today, stabilized does not mean that the patient has gotten better at all. It means that the hospital has determined that the illness won't get any worse.

A man was shocked at the treatment his mother received from a hospital. His mother had suffered a stroke and it was apparent to her son that she was still gravely ill. He felt that the hospital should keep her until she was "stabilized" and ready to go home. The hospital said she had to go. It was the hospital's opinion that she would not have another stroke and by their definition, she was "stabilized" and ready to be discharged.

Under the law, the hospital had the right to discharge his mother. She was discharged in a semi-conscious state, on a catheter, and with a feeding tube going into her stomach.

The remaining two possible methods of payment are Medicaid and private insurance.

Medicaid This health care system is funded by both the state and federal government. It is only available to the financially needy. Unlike Medicare, there are no deductibles. It pays when nothing else will.

Private insurance (such as HMOs and Blue Cross/Blue Shield) There are numerous health care plans which people can buy or which are provided by employers to pay for hospital care. Most private insurers now have a form of DRGs that they use to limit costs.

Taking Home a Chronically Ill Person

Regardless of who pays for the hospital, one thing is certain—hospitals are no longer places to get better. Once the patient is stabilized, the family must quickly find another place to care for him. At that point, there are usually only two options left: take the sick person home or put him in a nursing home.

When the sick person's illness or disability takes a mild form, home care may be a viable option for a while. But what happens when he cannot feed or clothe himself or take care of bodily functions without assistance? What if he is incontinent, in pain, depressed, unruly, or hostile? What happens when he cannot be left alone during waking hours? When he must be lifted from a bed to a wheelchair to the toilet and back?

What about the daughter who can't leave the house for twenty minutes because her mother might fall or set the house on fire? There is a saying about dealing with chronically ill people at home: Dealing with someone who is chronically ill eventually makes healthy people chronically ill. The care giver becomes a virtual prisoner in the house. The world closes down. Life as it was before the illness is gone completely.

And who is the care giver? The burdens of caring for our aging population fall disproportionately on women. It is usually the wife, daughter or daughter-in-law who sacrifices her way of life to take care of the chronically ill family member. Often she has sole responsibility in this difficult task. Her life takes a back seat to the needs of the sick person who requires care twenty-four hours a day. She may quit a job and give up all her other activities outside the home. The stress on her is enormous.

The situation affects members of the family not directly responsible for giving care. Families have been known to fall apart over taking care of mother or father. Some marriages are driven to the brink of divorce by the tremendous pressure of coping with the problem.

While the ideal of caring for an incapacitated family member at home is what every loving family aspires to, the realities of the situation are often so difficult that no amount of love, sacrifice, or denial can make it work.

What is left is the last viable, though often least desired, alternative: placement in a nursing home.

The Nursing Home

Nursing homes provide basically three types of care. They are:

- Medically necessary care (which in many ways approximates hospital care), for which Medicare will pay.

- Skilled nursing care which provides patients with continuous care and assistance by nurses and other professionals.

- Intermediate care for those who need help with everyday routine activities.

Medicare or other types of medical insurance plans will not pay for skilled nursing care or intermediate care since they are considered custodial care. The yearly cost for this kind of care can run as high as $60,000 in the northeast and west coast to $25,000 in the south, southwest and midwest. Many people have the mistaken idea that there exists some system or institution which will pay these bills.

People sometimes assume that the Veterans' Administration will pay for veterans who need custodial care. They rarely pay unless care is required because of a service-related illness or injury.

So how do people manage when confronted by an overwhelmingly confusing financial dilemma?

Who Pays — How the System Works

Few people want to escape reasonable financial responsibility for unfortunate circumstances in their own lives. Most people are more than willing to pay their fair share. But in every situation, there comes a point when enough is enough. The central issue in preserving a family's wellbeing is the ability to have a measure of control when a catastrophic illness hits.

Make no mistake about it: If families do not take steps early on to protect their assets from the consequences of a long-term illness, they *will* lose control. When that happens, there may be little or nothing left to provide for the surviving spouse and their offspring.

So we go back again to the question: Who pays for long term nursing home care?

The answer is shocking.

- Private health insurance companies will not pay for custodial care.
- The Veterans' Administration, in most cases, will not pay.
- Health Maintenance Organizations (HMOs) or related insurance plans will not pay.
- Medicare will not pay.

In fact, there are *only three* sources to pay for long-term nursing home care:

- Cash
- Medicaid
- Nursing home insurance.

Cash At a national average cost of $25,000 a year for nursing home care, a recent American Association of Retired Persons (AARP) poll found that an average family's life savings would be wiped out within nine months.

Medicaid No one likes to apply for public assistance. It is one of the great ironies that the very system that older Americans have struggled for years to avoid, for many will be the only means to pay for nursing home care.

Nursing home insurance Insurance companies are beginning to offer plans that will pay certain amounts towards daily custodial care for a period of years. These policies may be the right answer for those who fear the financial consequences of nursing home confinement but want to maintain control for as long as possible.

If you understand how these systems work, your life savings need not be wiped out. It *is* possible to protect your savings for a surviving spouse or to take care of your children should they need assistance in the future.

It's time to get educated. Let's look at the law and see how the law looks at your assets.

The following information by nature must state only general principles because the federal government allows each state a certain amount of flexibility in applying the law. Be sure to refer to the tables to see how your state interprets the regulations. Also, regulations change constantly. Be sure to call your local Department of Public Welfare to see if the rules have changed.

The earlier you begin to plan, the better.

3

THE BASICS —
UNDERSTANDING MEDICAID

THE BASICS — UNDERSTANDING MEDICAID

Assets

Under the current system, there are two factors that determine eligibility for public assistance: assets and income.

Assets: Definition — everything you own that has value.

That definition seems simple enough. Medicaid, however, divides assets into three categories. Don't try to make sense out of why a particular asset falls into one category and not another. No one ever said that the Medicaid program was rational. In fact, it sometimes appears that Medicaid is as confused as we are in trying to figure out what they will take and what they will let us keep.

The three groups of assets are: countable, non-countable and inaccessible.

Countable assets

Countable assets: These are things that Medicaid wants you to spend to zero before financial assistance is available.

They include:
- Cash over $2,000 (in most states)
- Stocks
- Bonds
- IRAs
- Keoghs

- Certificates of deposit
- Single premium deferred annuities
- Treasury notes and treasury bills
- Savings bonds
- Investment property
- Whole life insurance above a certain amount
- Vacation homes
- Second vehicles
- Every other asset that is not specifically listed as non-countable is included in this list.

These are things that are in jeopardy when catastrophic illness strikes. In order to qualify for Medicaid the applicant must in effect be BANKRUPT.

Non-countable assets

Non-countable assets (also called exempt assets) Believe it or not, these things can be worth hundreds of thousands of dollars but Medicaid has chosen not to count them in determining elegibility. These assets are not in jeopardy.

They include:
- A house used as a primary residence (in most states this includes two-and three-family homes)
- An amount of cash (usually $2,000) (see chart page 164)
- A car
- Personal jewelry
- Household effects

- A pre-paid funeral
- A burial account (not to exceed $2,500 in most states)
- Term life insurance policies (as opposed to whole life) which have no cash surrender value. (see chart page 178 for whole life policies)

See chart on page 168 to determine what assets your state allows you to keep.

Life insurance is generally divided into two groups: whole life and term. Whole life has a cash value which increases the longer you hold the policy. Although the insurance lapses when you stop paying, you receive cash value back. This is called the policy's surrender value.

Term insurance never builds up a cash value, but is worth only the face amount on the policy and then only when you die. Coverage stops when you stop paying. Most states allow you to keep unlimited term insurance when applying for Medicaid but only a limited amount of whole life insurance. See chart on page 168.

Inaccessible assets

Inaccessible assets These are countable assets which have been made unavailable to Medicaid. To put it bluntly, *if you can't get them, they can't get them.*

Assets are made inaccessible by

1) Giving them away,
2) Holding them in Medicaid trusts (see below),
3) Holding them in certain types of joint accounts (see page 86),
4) An involuntary situation where the person who owns the assets is too incapacitated to get access to them (see page 94).

Holding assets in Medicaid trusts

Medicaid Trusts

There are two kinds of trusts to consider: revocable and irrevocable. The difference between the two is that the first can be changed after it is set up, the second can't.

A **revocable trust** is a legal instrument that you set up to hold assets. There must be at least one trustee and one or more beneficiaries. A trustee is simply the person who makes the decisions for the trust. The beneficiary is the person who gets the benefit of the assets in the trust. Since you make the trust, you make the rules that the trustee must follow. If you don't like the trust, you can change it or do away with it. That's why it is called revocable. A revocable trust also acts as a will. The rules you make can include who gets your money and under what conditions after you die. While you are alive you receive the benefits. This kind of trust is useful in protecting your house (see Chapter 7), but it will *not* protect countable assets.

An **irrevocable trust,** like a revocable trust, is a legal instrument that you set up to hold assets. Like a revocable trust, there must be one or more trustees and one or more beneficiaries. The definition of a trustee and beneficiary are the same as above. You can make the same rules. The difference is that once you've made the rules you can't change them. By making it irrevocable you give up the power to modify or do away with the trust. Simply put, you lose control.

The only trust that will protect countable assets is an irrevocable trust but *only* one that limits the amount of discretion a trustee has. These are called Medicaid Trusts.

Congress passed a law that took effect in 1986 restricting the use of irrevocable trusts. It says that if you set up an irrevocable trust, name yourself as a beneficiary, and give the power to your trustee to give you all, some or none of the income and assets, Medicaid will assume your trustee will make all the income and principal available to you and thus the nursing home. It doesn't matter that your trustee can say, "I have the power to refuse to give the nursing home any money." Medicaid won't buy it.

The trust has to be set up in such a way as to limit the power of the trustee. If, for example, the trustee has no power to give you the assets, but only to hold them, Medicaid can't get them. It's the old principle, "If I can't get them, you can't get them."

Example: An irrevocable trust that *doesn't* protect assets

A husband and wife set up The ABC Family Trust. They name their son as the trustee and themselves as beneficiaries. They give the trustee the power to give them all, some or none of the principal and income. The day a parent/beneficiary goes into the nursing home is the day the "snapshot"* is taken of the couple's assets. Since they gave discretion over the assets and income to the trustee, Medicaid assumes that the trustee will use his full discretion and make the assets and income available to the parent. In other words, the assets are considered countable, available, and therefore subject to division just as if they weren't in trust.

* For a detailed explanation of "snapshots" and how Medicaid treats assets held by spouses, see pages 29-32.

Example: An irrevocable trust that *does* protect assets

A husband and wife set up The ABC Family Trust with the same trustee and beneficiaries. This time they don't give any power to the trustee to give them the assets, only the power to hold them in trust while they generate income. The day a parent goes into the nursing home is the day the snapshot is taken of their assets. However, this time the assets in the trust are not in the snapshot because the trustee cannot make them available to the parent.

WARNING: There are thousands of Medicaid qualifying trusts that were set up prior to 1986 which were made invalid by the law Congress passed that year. Today, none of these trusts will protect assets even though they were legal and effective when set up. If your trust was established before 1986, be sure to contact your attorney to make the appropriate changes.

REMEMBER: In defining non-countable assets, specifics vary from state to state. Be sure to check the chart on page 168 to see how assets are classified in your locale. Also, regulations change so be sure to check with your local welfare agency when planning or filling out an application for Medicaid.

The Spousal Impoverishment Act

The Spousal Impoverishment Act (SIA) supposedly protects a stay-at-home spouse (the person not going into the nursing home) by allowing him or her to keep certain amounts of assets and income.

As of October 1, 1989, Medicaid treats marital assets this way:

Step 1 — Medicaid determines the day a spouse goes into a nursing home or medical institution.

Step 2 — Medicaid requires that the couple list all their countable assets regardless of whose name they are in, who earned them or how long they've been in either's name.

Step 3 — Medicaid takes a snapshot, a picture of the combined assets on the day the spouse goes into the nursing home or medical institution.

Step 4 — The stay-at-home spouse is then allowed to keep one-half of the total amount of the assets in the snapshot, but **not less than $12,000 or more than $60,000.** (This figure will go up annually.)

Example: Curtis is going into a nursing home on June 1. He and his wife Helen, have total assets of $20,000, $15,000 of which is in his IRA. Medicaid will take a snapshot of the couple's combined assets on June 1. Helen will be allowed to keep one-half of $20,000. Since half of $20,000 is $10,000, she will be allowed to keep $12,000, the minimum.

If Curtis and Helen had $150,000, Helen would not be allowed to keep half ($75,000) but only $60,000, the maximum.

To make matters a little more confusing, although the principles here are consistent across the board, the dollar amounts may vary from state to state. The law allows each state to set the amount the stay-at-home spouse may keep between a minimum of $12,000 and a maximum of $60,000. Here's how that works:

Your state may decide to raise the floor on the amount a stay-at-home spouse may keep of their joint assets. Rather than a floor of $12,000, your state may allow $40,000. What happens in our example when the floor is raised to $40,000? Helen would be allowed to keep the entire $20,000 because their state raised the floor from $12,000 to $40,000 (see chart page 158).

An application for Medicaid is usually not made on the day the spouse goes into the nursing home. Whether he or she will be able to qualify is determined by using the method described on page 29.

If assets have to be spent down by the institutionalized spouse in order to qualify, the application for Medicaid may not take place for months. Regardless of what the total assets are on the day he applies, the stay-at-home spouse's share will always be determined on the day of the snapshot.

Example: Joel and Esther have combined countable assets of $100,000 at the time Esther goes into a nursing home on January 1. The snapshot is taken on January 1. Joel's spousal share (the amount he is allowed to keep) is $50,000. Unless Esther buys non-countable assets or otherwise protects her money (see page 23) she will have to spend $48,000 on her care ($50,000 minus $2,000, the maximum assets she can keep.)

Let's say that Joel applies for Medicaid for his wife when there is $70,000 left of countable assets. All Esther would have to spend is $18,000. Why? Because Medicaid goes back to January 1 to determine what Joel's share is ($50,000.) This amount deducted from $70,000 leaves $20,000 that Esther will have to spend. She is allowed to keep $2,000 of that amount.

Income

Definition — Income is all the money you receive from any source. Like countable assets, it is in jeopardy.

The money may come from one or a combination of the following:
- Social security
- Interest and investments
- Trusts
- Rental units
- Help from family members
- Pensions
- Annuities
- In a nutshell, you name it, if you get it, Medicaid wants it.

Income eligibility is quite simple. In most states, if the person who is going into the nursing home has monthly income that exceeds the nursing home bill, he pays the nursing home directly. (See chart pages 160-161 showing what states set limits on monthly income.)

If that person's monthly income is less than the nursing home bill, Medicaid has him give it to the home and Medicaid makes up the difference. Most, if not all, of your income, regardless of where it comes from, for whatever reason you get it, will have to go to the nursing home.

Most states allow single people to hold back

- a personal needs allowance (see chart page 162)
- a home maintenance allowance if planning to go home (see chart page 163)
- a monthly premium to pay for medical insurance.

Income rules do not apply to the stay-at-home spouse. She is free to continue working and keep her salary and other monthly income (like social security.) In addition the state usually allows the spouse to keep her half of the assets that generate income such as dividends, rent, etc.

The law requires states to set a specified amount the stay-at-home spouse may keep from total joint income. As of October 1, 1989, the minimum is $815 per month, the maximum $1,500. The states have discretion in setting the amount within those limits. The well spouse has the opportunity to increase the state-set amount if she can show that her housing expenses are unusually high.

Example: Dennis and Eleanor's only income is $1,200 a month in social security. Of that, $1,000 is the husband's, $200 is his wife's. If Dennis goes into a nursing home he will be allowed to make the following deductions from his $1,000.

- a personal needs account (approximately $50 a month in most states; See chart page 162).

- *the premium for his medex or equivalent insurance policy that pays the deductibles on his Medicare policy.*
- *$615 monthly to supplement his wife's $200 a month since the minimum she is provided from the spousal income is $815.*

Remember, Eleanor's income is unaffected. If she is working, all her salary remains hers. She does not have to make a contribution to Dennis' nursing home expense.

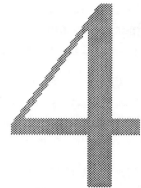

HOW TO PROTECT ASSETS WHEN THERE'S TIME TO PLAN

HOW TO PROTECT ASSETS WHEN THERE'S TIME TO PLAN

When a diagnosis is made early and the illness is expected to progress slowly, the family has time to plan. For protecting assets, this is the time to start.

The key to protection is knowing what assets and income are in jeopardy and what the critical deadlines are for transferring them. In the preceding chapter, we identified which assets and income are in jeopardy.

Our goal is to take countable assets (those that have to be spent to zero) (see page 22), and make them either non-countable, and therefore protected (see page 23), or inaccessible which means that Medicaid can't get them (see page 24). In the following chapter, we will look at the options available to people in different situations

Remember: The key to protecting assets when you have time to plan is understanding the rules about disqualification.

The Disqualification Period — 30 Months

When a transfer of a countable asset is made to the inaccessible category (see page 24), the person making the transfer is disqualified for a period of months. Read and memorize the following rule:

If you transfer countable assets for less than fair market value (see pages 80-85) within 30 months of

applying for Medicaid or going into a nursing home or a medical institution, it is presumed that you did it to have Medicaid pay the expense of institutional care.

Example: Sam transfers all his savings ($50,000) to his son on January 1, 1990. He goes into a nursing home on January 1, 1991. Since he gave his money away within 30 months of being institutionalized, and he will not qualify for Medicaid until either 18 months has passed (30 months minus the 12 months that passed between the date of transfer and his entry into the home) or until he has used up on nursing home bills all the transferred money.

If assets are to be protected, it is imperative that a transfer be made at least 30 months before the day the applicant goes into the nursing home or applies for Medicaid.

This is especially important if the nursing home resident went in before October 1989 (when the disqualification period was increased to 30 months for all states). Since he would be under his state's old law, there may be severe penalties for applying for Medicaid within the old disqualification time. Never apply for Medicaid benefits until after the entire disqualification period (old and new) has passed. For a more complete explanation see pages 80-85.

At this point we have covered the general principles involved in protecting assets. Now let's get down to specifics.

There is no single course of action that best suits every situation. To demonstrate the various options, we will explore several examples. One of these will closely fit your own situation. The examples cover asset protection for

- Spouses
- Offspring and parents
- Offspring and single parent
- Siblings
- Nieces/nephews and aunts/uncles
- Grandchildren and grandparents
- Unrelated people

In each example, we will consider the pros and cons of all the options available in these particular circumstances. After reviewing the choices, we will determine which option best suits the needs of the people involved.

All examples assume that the family has at least 30 months before nursing home confinement.

Spouses

This example deals with a spouse who may need nursing home care in the future (at least 30 months) and how his family can help protect the family's assets. The Andrews have a close and trusting relationship with daughter Susan, but not with son Bill.

NAME:	Mr. and Mrs. Andrews
AGE:	husband 65
	wife 65
ASSETS:	house $150,000 (jointly held, no mortgage)
	savings (joint) $50,000
	(includes wife's inheritance of $10,000)
INSURANCE:	husband has two insurance policies, a whole
	life policy with a face value of $10,000 and
	a cash surrender value of $2,000, and a
	term policy worth $25,000.
INCOME:	joint, from savings $4,000/year
	social security: husband $650/month
	wife $300/month
HEALTH:	husband, early Alzheimer's
	wife, good
FAMILY:	two adult children, Bill and Susan

The goal is to take countable assets and move them to the non-countable or inaccessible column. Here is how the assets would be categorized at the time of the Alzheimer's diagnosis before steps are taken to protect them:

non-countable	countable	inaccessible
house term policy	joint savings $50,000 whole life insurance policy	none presently

What Happens When the Husband and Wife Don't Plan

If assets remain in the countable column, they will have to be spent on nursing home care, subject to the Spousal Impoverishment Act (see page 29), before the husband qualifies for financial assistance. If these assets are transferred to the inaccessible column within 30 months of going into a nursing home, Medicaid presumes that he is trying to hide the assets.

Here's what will happen if the assets remain exactly as they appear above:

On the day the husband goes into the nursing home, Medicaid will take a snapshot (see page 29) of the couple's assets regardless of whose name they are in. Since the countable assets were not shifted to other categories, the wife will be allowed to keep only a specified amount. That figure is arrived at by applying a somewhat confusing formula: She may keep no less than $12,000 OR one half of their combined total assets up to a limit of $60,000, whichever is greater.

Looking at the Andrews chart, we see that their joint funds are $50,000. Half of that is $25,000. Since $25,000 is greater than $12,000 and less than $60,000 she is allowed to keep $25,000.

Here's what happens if their savings account is $15,000 instead of $50,000. One half of $15,000 is $7,500. Because $7,500 is less than $12,000, she gets to keep the greater amount ($12,000) since that's the *minimum* the law allows.

What would have happened if their savings account had been $200,000? One half is $100,000. Because $100,000 is greater than $60,000, she gets to keep only $60,000 since that is the *maximum* the law allows.

If you are feeling confused, there's nothing wrong with you. This concept can be difficult to grasp. Go back and read the example again.

Individual states are allowed by law to raise the amount the stay-at-home spouse may keep.

What happens if the state where the Andrews live raises to $40,000 the minimum amount that she could keep? Our chart shows total countable assets of $50,000. One half of $50,000 is $25,000. Because the floor is now $40,000, the wife in our example gets to keep not one half or $25,000 but $40,000 of their $50,000 in joint assets.

Now, let's say that the couple had $150,000 in joint assets. One half is $75,000. Because $75,000 is more than the ceiling of $60,000, she would keep only $60,000. In this case, the floor ($40,000) is not used.

What Happens When the Husband and Wife Have Time to Plan

Let's look at the various options we might use to protect those assets if the Andrews have 30 months or more before nursing home confinement.

Remember: Assets may be protected (made inaccessible) by

Option 1 Giving them away

Option 2 Holding them in trust

Option 3 Holding them in certain types of joint accounts

Option 4 An involuntary situation where the applicant is too sick to gain access (not applicable in the Andrews' situation)

After examining each option, we will see which is best suited for this specific situation.

Option 1A Giving away assets — one spouse to the other

The law *prior* to November, 1989 A good example of how fast Medicaid law is changing is the November 1989 revision of the regulation covering spousal transfer of assets. Prior to that time, the only spouse prohibited from transferring assets was the one being institutionalized. As long as the stay-at-home spouse had countable assets in her name for at least 30 months, she was free to transfer them without penalty even if the transfer occurred the day before the snapshot.

Mr. Andrews could have taken his name and social security number off all the countable assets. The account would then be in the name of his wife only or, if she wished, she could add a son or daughter as a co-holder.

Let's say thirty months have passed from the day of the transfer. Under the old law, if Mr. Andrews were institutionalized, his wife would have been free to transfer the assets to the children as long as it was done before the day of the snapshot. Since the wife was not being institutionalized, her assets (those in her name for at least 30 months) could be transferred without penalty.

The option of giving all the countable assets to the healthy spouse for the purpose of protecting them from Medicaid is no longer viable.

The law *after* November, 1989 Mrs. Andrews has had all the countable assets in her name alone for at least 30 months. Her husband is going into a nursing home tomorrow. Under the new law, if she tries to transfer the assets to her children, Medicaid will consider the transfer as if her husband had made it: He will be disqualified for 30 months or until the countable assets are spent.

The option of giving all the countable assets to the healthy spouse for the purpose of protecting them from Medicaid is no longer viable.

Option 1B Giving away assets — To the offspring

Here's a little wisdom to ponder: Never give your assets to your children unless you are absolutely, positively willing to stake your life on the belief that they will give them back or make them available to you when you ask.

Here's what you want to avoid:

• The children spending them because they "thought it was a gift."

• Your son's or daughter's spouse (whom you never liked in the first place) getting your assets in a divorce.

• Your son or daughter losing the money in a bad business deal.

A rule of thumb in determining whether your offspring should be the choice to hold and protect your assets: If you have to think more than one half of one second before you answer "yes," forget the whole idea. On the other hand, if you do have a close and trusting relationship with your offspring, you can enlist their help in protecting your assets.

Option 2 Holding assets in trust

There are different kinds of trusts to consider. For a complete explanation, before continuing please go back and read pages 25-28.

Example: An irrevocable trust that *doesn't* protect assets

The Andrews set up The Andrews Family Trust naming their children as trustees and themselves as beneficiaries. They give the trustees the power to give them all or some or none of the principal and income. The day Mr. Andrews goes into the nursing home is the day a snapshot is taken of their assets (see page 29). Since they gave discretion over the assets and income to the trustees, Medicaid assumes that the trustees will use their power and make the assets and income available to the parents. In other words, the assets are considered countable and therefore available, subject to the Spousal Impoverishment Act (see page 29).

Example: An irrevocable trust that *does* protect assets

The Andrews set up The Andrews Family Trust with their children as trustees and themselves as beneficiaries. This time, however, they don't give any power to the trustees to give them the assets, only the power to hold them in trust while they generate income for them. The day Mr. Andrews goes into the nursing home is the day the snapshot is taken of their assets. However, this time the assets in the trust are not in the snapshot because the trustees cannot make them available to their parents. However, Medicaid may get the income (see pages 32-34, 95-99).

Here's what the Andrews can do to protect their assets:

Plan A Establish an irrevocable trust like the second example above; OR

Plan B Establish an irrevocable trust like the second example above but naming a third person as a beneficiary and giving the trustee power to distribute funds to that third person.

The Andrews establish the Andrews Family Trust, making it irrevocable. They name themselves as beneficiaries along with a third person, such as their daughter Susan. They name a fourth party as trustee and give him control over the assets. The trust allows the trustee to give only Susan the principal at any time, never Mr. and Mrs. Andrews. The Andrews can only get money through Susan, the third beneficiary. If either of the Andrews goes into a nursing home, the principal will be protected since the trustee never had discretion to give principal to either of them.

Plan C Establish a revocable trust naming Mr. and Mrs. Andrews as beneficiaries but specifying that the trust becomes irrevocable if either one of them goes into a nursing home or has a long-term illness.

Which Plan is best?

Plan A means that the Andrews give up full control of

the assets well before the husband goes into the home. This is the same as giving them away. Also, they can't get their principal.

Plan B still means that the Andrews give up full control of their assets. However, the trustee can give the assets to a third person who in turn could make them available to the Andrews.

During the time that the Andrews are not in a nursing home, they will have to get their assets through that third party (such as a son or daughter or close friend).

If Mr. Andrews goes into a home, the trustee can still get money to Mrs. Andrews by using the above method.

However you slice it though, this trust takes control away from the Andrews. If the Andrews do not feel comfortable with giving this power to a relative or close friend, this option doesn't work for them.

Plan C means that the Andrews' assets are countable and available to Medicaid for 30 months. Why? Because revocable trusts don't protect countable assets.

The trust in Plan C only becomes irrevocable when there's a long-term illness or nursing home confinement. Therefore 30 months must expire before the assets are protected. This plan is useful only for people with a great deal of money who can easily afford to pay privately for 30 months. The Andrews can't.

Which plan is best?

If a trust is to be used, Plan B is best because it protects the assets while still making them available through a third person. The key is that the third person *must* be trustworthy.

Option 3 Holding assets in a joint account

The Andrews, like most couples, hold their assets in an "either/or" savings account. "Either" the husband "or" the wife can gain access to the account without the other's signature. Medicaid considers this type of account available when determining countable assets.

There's another type of account that the Andrews could open that requires *both* signatures. This is called an "and" account because both his "and" her signatures are required for either one to get the money.

In most states (be sure to check with your Department of Public Welfare), an "and" account is protected from being spent on a chronic care facility or nursing home if the stay-at-home spouse refuses to co-sign the check or withdrawal slip to give the ill spouse access to the account. It remains inaccessible until the spouse in the nursing home dies.

If the Andrews have a savings account that requires two signatures, Mrs. Andrews can make the entire amount inaccessible by simply refusing to co-sign the withdrawal slip.

Drawbacks:

1) If Mrs. Andrews dies while her husband is in the nursing home, the entire balance becomes available to the nursing home. If he is on Medicaid, he will immediately be disqualified because he now has money.

2) Although the money is frozen until Mr. Andrews dies, it also is unavailable to Mrs. Andrews. Why? Because Mrs. Andrews needs her husband's signature to take money from the account. Any withdrawal would immediately be considered countable and available to pay the nursing home. (Medicaid would find out about the transfer since most states request a periodic update from the applicant. Since Mr. Andrews declared this account on his application, Medicaid would be on the lookout for any changes in status.)

The above option of holding money in an "and" account is not practical if you have 30 months or more to plan. It can be useful when you are in a crisis situation (see page 86).

Life Insurance In reviewing how the Andrews' assets are divided, you will notice that his term policy is non-countable and therefore can be kept. Not so with his whole life policy since the face value, not the cash surrender value, exceeds a certain face amount. See chart on page 168. It is suggested that Mr. Andrews transfer ownership of the policy to either his wife or one of the children to make it inaccessible.

WHICH OF OUR OPTIONS IS BEST?

Option 2, Plan B — holding money with a third person as beneficiary is the best alternative other than giving the money outright to the Andrews' children.

Here is how the transferred assets line up:

non-countable	countable	inaccessible
house term policy	0	whole life insurance policy now owned by wife or Susan assets in irrevocable trust

A note about the Andrews' house:

It makes no sense to protect the Andrews' money without protecting the house too. Even though it is a non-countable asset (Medicaid allows the Andrews to keep it while receiving financial assistance), they will place a lien on the house upon the death of both spouses. Please refer to Chapter 7 for a complete explanation of how to protect a house.

Offspring and Parents

This example deals with elderly parents who are *both* in frail health. The Rossis have a close and trusting relationship with their children; therefore the children are available to help their parents protect their assets.

NAME:	Mr. and Mrs. Rossi
CHILDREN:	Maria and Joseph
PARENTS' AGE:	husband, 82
	wife, 79
ASSETS:	two-family house, $150,000
	savings bonds 25,000
	stocks 30,000
	savings and CDs 45,000
INCOME:	husband $600/month social security
	$500/month pension
	wife $250 /month social security
	$150/month pension
	joint $350/month investment interest
HEALTH:	husband Parkinson's disease, early stage
	wife fair health

Our goal is to protect countable assets from being spent on Mr. Rossi's expected nursing home confinement.

Before continuing, go back to page 29 and review the Spousal Impoverishment Act.

Here's how the assets line up before steps are taken to protect them:

non-countable	countable	inaccessible
2-family house	savings and CDs $45,000 stocks $30,000 savings bonds $25,000	none presently

What Happens When the Family Has Time to Plan

Let's look at the various options to protect assets when Mr. Rossi has 30 months or more before nursing home confinement.

Remember: assets may be protected (made inaccessible) by

Option 1 Giving away assets

    A — One spouse to the other

    B — To the offspring

Option 2 Holding them in trust

Option 3 Holding them in certain types of joint accounts

Option 4 An involuntary situation where the applicant is too sick to gain access (not applicable in the Rossi's situation)

After examining each option, we will see which is best suited for this specific situation.

Option 1A Giving away assets — one spouse to the other

A good example of how fast Medicaid law is changing is the November 1989 revision of the regulation covering spousal transfer of assets. Prior to that time, the only spouse prohibited from transferring assets was the one being institutionalized. As long as the stay-at-home spouse had countable assets in her name for at least 30 months, she was free to transfer them without penalty even if the transfer occurred the day before the snapshot.

The law prior to November, 1989 Mr Rossi could have taken his name and social security number off all the countable assets. The account would then be in the name of his wife only or, if she wished, he could add a son or daughter as a co-holder.

Let's say thirty months have passed from the day of the transfer. Under the old law, if Mr. Rossi were institutionalized, his wife would have been free to transfer the assets to the children as long as the transfer was completed before the day of the snapshot. Since the wife was not being institutionalized, her assets (those in her name for at least 30 months) could be transferred without penalty.

The law after November, 1989 Mrs. Rossi has had all the countable assets in her name alone for at least 30 months. Her husband is going into a nursing home tomorrow. Under the new law, if she tries to transfer the assets to her children, Medicaid will consider the transfer as if her husband had made it: He will be disqualified for 30 months or until the countable assets are spent.

Option 1B: Giving away assets — To the offspring

Since the Rossis have a close relationship with Maria and Joseph and trust their judgment, they may choose to transfer all the assets to them. As long as 30 months pass from the date of the transfer, the assets will not be counted in determining Medicaid eligibility for Mr. Rossi.

Drawbacks

1) Either or both of the Rossi children may get a divorce. Most states would consider the parents' assets part of the offsprings' marital property subject to division.

2) Maria or Joseph might die, which means that their spouse could inherit the assets being held for their parents.

To avoid these problems, both should sign an agreement with their spouses stating that the assets are being held for their parents and are not part of the marital property. Also, each should make a will specifying that the money they are holding is to be placed in a trust for their parent's use. The trust should state that upon the death of both parents, the assets will be given to whomever the parents wish.

Option 2 Holding assets in trust

There are different kinds of trusts to consider. For a complete explanation before continuing please go back and read pages 25-28.

Example: An irrevocable trust that *doesn't* protect assets

The husband and wife set up The Rossi Family Trust. They name their son and daughter as trustees and themselves as beneficiaries. They give the trustees the power to give them all, some or none of the principal and income. The day Mr. Rossi goes into the nursing home is the day the snapshot (see page 29) is taken of the couples assets. Since they gave discretion over the assets and income to the trustees, Medicaid assumes that the trustees will use their discretion to make the assets and income available to their parents. In other words, the assets are considered countable and therefore available subject to the Spousal Impoverishment Act (see page 29).

Example: An irrevocable trust that *does* protect assets

Mr. and Mrs. Rossi set up The Rossi Family Trust with the same trustees and beneficiaries. This time, however, they don't give any power to the trustees to give them the assets, only the power to hold assets in trust while they generate income for them. The day Mr. Rossi goes into the nursing

home is the day the snapshot is taken of their assets. However, now the assets in the trust are not in the snapshot because the trustees cannot make them available to the their parents.

Here's what the Rossis could do to protect their assets:

Plan A Establish an irrevocable trust like the second example above; OR

Plan B Establish an irrevocable trust naming one of their children as a third beneficiary and giving the trustees power to distribute funds to that person (see page 47).

During the time that the Rossis are not in a nursing home they will have to get their assets through that third party. If Mr. Rossi goes into a home, the trustee can still get money to Mrs. Rossi by using the above method.

Plan C Establish a revocable trust naming the Rossis as beneficiaries but specifying that the trust becomes irrevocable if either one of them goes into a nursing home or has a long-term illness.

Which of the above choices is best?

Plan A means that the Rossis give up full control of the assets well before the husband goes into the home. This is the same as giving away assets. It also means that they can't get their principal.

Plan B still means that the Rossis give up full control of their assets. However, the trustee can give the assets to third parties, such as Maria and/or Joseph. During the time that neither of the Rossis is in a nursing home, the trustee, who has the power to give principal to third parties, gives money to Maria. She, in turn, can make a gift of the money to her parents. If Mr. Rossi goes into a home, the trustee could still get money to Mrs. Rossi by using the above method. However you slice it, though, this trust still takes control away from the Rossis.

Plan C means that the Rossi's assets are countable for 30 months. Why? Because revocable trusts don't protect countable assets. The trust in Plan C only becomes irrevocable when there's a long term illness or nursing home confinement. Therefore 30 months must expire before the assets are protected. This option is useful only for people with a great deal of money who can easily afford to pay privately for 30 months. The Rossis can't.

Plan B is the best choice because the Rossis have a close and trusting relationship with their offspring. One caution: In some states only one of the children can be the third beneficiary; if both are listed the trust might be invalid. Check the law in the state where you live.

Option 3 Holding assets in joint accounts

The Rossis, like most couples, hold their assets in an "either/or" savings account. "Either" the husband "or" the wife can gain access to the account without the other's signature. Medicaid considers this type of account available when determining countable assets. In other words, one half of the assets would have to be spent on the nursing home.

There's another type of account that the Rossis could open that requires *both* signatures. This is called an "and" account because both his "and" her signature are required for either one to get the money (see page 86).

In most states (make sure you check your local Department of Public Welfare), an "and" account is protected from being spent on a nursing home if the stay-at-home spouse refuses to co-sign the check or withdrawal slip to give the ill spouse access to the account. It remains inaccessible until the spouse in the nursing home dies.

In our example, if any of the Rossi's investments required two signatures, Mrs. Rossi could make the entire amount inaccessible by simply refusing to co-sign the withdrawal slip.

Again: Because regulations vary from state to state, be sure to check with your local welfare office to be sure an "and" account is considered inaccessible.

Drawbacks

1) If Mrs. Rossi dies while her husband is in the nursing home, the entire balance will become available to the nursing home. If he was on Medicaid, he will immediately be disqualified because he now has money.

2) Although the money is frozen until Mr. Rossi dies, it also is unavailable to his wife. Why? Because Mrs. Rossi needs her husband's signature to take money out of the account. Any withdrawal would immediately be considered countable and available to the nursing home. (Medicaid would find out about the transfer since most states request periodic updates from the applicant. Since Mr. Rossi declared this account on his application, Medicaid would be on the lookout for any changes in status.)

Because of these drawbacks and the fact that the Rossis have at least 30 months to plan, the option of holding money in an "and" account is not the best choice for them. (An "and" account can be useful when you are in a crisis situation; see page 86.)

WHICH OF OUR OPTIONS IS BEST?

Either Option 1B, giving away assets — To the offspring or Option 2, Plan B, holding assets in an irrevocable trust with a third beneficiary would be the best solutions.

Here is how the transferred assets line up:

non-countable	countable	inaccessible
2-family house	0	assets are placed in an irrevocable trust or assets are given outright to offspring

A note about the Rossi's house: It makes no sense to protect the Rossi's money without protecting the house too. Even though it is a non-countable asset (Medicaid allows the Andrews to keep it while receiving financial assistance), a lien will be placed on the house upon the death of both spouses. Please refer to Chapter 7 for a complete explanation of how to protect a house.

Offspring and Single Parent

This example is used to show how children can help a widowed parent who is too ill to handle her own assets.

NAME:	Mrs. Stein, Mr. Stein deceased
CHILDREN:	one daughter, Ruth (married)
AGE:	86
ASSETS:	savings $75,000
INCOME:	social security $400/month
	investments $500/month
HEALTH:	early stage Alzheimer's

Our goal is to protect countable assets from being spent on Mrs. Stein's nursing home confinement.

Here's how the assets line up before steps are taken to protect them:

non-countable	countable	inaccessible
none	$75,000	none presently

If assets remain in the countable column, they will have to be spent on nursing home care before Mrs. Stein qualifies for financial assistance. If these assets are transferred to the inaccessible column within 30 months of going into a nursing home, Medicaid presumes that it was done to hide the assets.

Let's look at the various options we might use to protect those assets if Mrs. Stein has 30 months or more before nursing home confinement.

Remember: assets may be protected (made inaccessible) by

Option 1 Giving them away

Option 2 Holding them in trust

Option 3 Holding them in certain types of joint accounts

Option 4 An involuntary situation where the applicant is too sick to gain access (not applicable in the Stein's situation)

After examining each option, we will see which is best suited for this specific situation.

Option 1 Giving away assets

If her savings account is held jointly with her daughter, Mrs. Stein can simply take off her name and social security number. If the account is in her name alone, the money can be transferred to an account with only her daughter's name and social security number. If Mrs. Stein can stay out of a nursing home for 30 months or more, the money is protected because she is only prohibited from receiving Medicaid benefits if she transfers the money within 30 months of entering the nursing home or applying for assistance.

Drawbacks

1) Ruth may die while holding her mother's money. Ruth can handle this by making a will which sets up a trust for her mother's benefit. She would have to choose a person to handle the trust (a trustee) and a person(s) who would get the money upon her mother's death.

2) Ruth may get divorced. Most states consider a couple's assets as joint property regardless of whose name is on them. Ruth should set up an agreement with her husband excluding her mother's assets from their joint property. If Ruth is single but is planning to get married, she should sign a pre-marital agreement excluding the assets in the event of a divorce.

Option 2 Holding assets in trust

There are different kinds of trusts to consider. For a complete explanation, before continuing please go back to pages 25-28.

Example: An irrevocable trust that *doesn't* protect assets

Mrs. Stein can set up The Stein Family Trust naming her daughter as trustee and herself as beneficiary. She gives Ruth the power to give her all, some or none of the principal and income. Since she gave discretion over the assets and income to the trustee, Medicaid assumes that the trustee will use her power and make the assets and income available to her mother. In other words, the assets are considered countable and therefore available (see page 22).

Example: An irrevocable trust that *does* protect assets

Mrs. Stein sets up The Stein Family Trust with the same trustee and beneficiary. This time, however, she doesn't give any power to the trustee to give her the assets, only the power to hold them in trust while they generate income for her. However, this time the assets in the trust are not available because the trustee has no authority to give them to her mother.

Here's what Mrs. Stein could do:

Plan A Establish an irrevocable trust like the second example above; OR

Plan B Establish a revocable trust naming herself as beneficiary but specifying that the trust becomes irrevocable if she goes into a nursing home or has a long-term illness.

Which option is best?

Plan A means that Mrs. Stein gives up full control of the assets well before she goes into the home. This is the same as giving assets away.

Plan B means that Mrs. Stein's assets are countable for 30 months because revocable trusts don't protect countable assets. The trust in Plan B only becomes irrevocable when there's a long-term illness or nursing home confinement. Therefore 30 months must expire before the assets are protected. This option is useful only for people with a great deal of money who can easily afford to pay privately for 30 months. Mrs. Stein can't.

If any trust is to be used, Plan A is the best choice because Mrs. Stein has a close and trusting relationship with her daughter.

Option 3 Holding assets in joint accounts

Mrs. Stein, like many widows, holds her assets in an "either/or" account with an offspring, in this case Ruth. Either the mother *"or"* the daughter can gain access to the account without the other's signature. Medicaid considers this type of account completely owned by Mrs. Stein unless she can prove otherwise. Why? Because the presumption is that the money is really Mrs. Stein's and her daughter's name is on the account for the sake of convenience (see page 86).

There's another type of account that Mrs. Stein could open that requires both signatures. This is called an "and" account because both hers *"and"* her daughter's signature are required for either one to get the money.

In most states (be sure to check your Department of Public Welfare), an "and" account is protected from being spent on a nursing home if the co-holder refuses to co-sign the check or withdrawal slip to give the ill person access to the account. The account remains inaccessible until the person in the nursing home dies.

In our example, if any of Mrs. Stein's investments required two signatures, Ruth could make the entire amount inaccessible by simply refusing to co-sign the withdrawal slip.

Drawback

Money held in an "and" account becomes vulnerable in two situations: First, the money becomes a countable asset to Mrs. Stein if Ruth dies first. Second, even though Ruth will probably outlive her mother, this money may be frozen until her mother dies because regulations vary from state to state. Be sure to check with your local welfare office to be sure an "and" account is considered inaccessible.

WHICH OF OUR OPTIONS IS BEST?

1) Giving away assets?
2) Holding assets in trust?
3) Holding assets jointly?

Option 1, giving assets away to her daughter, would be the best approach since mother and daughter have a close relationship and there are no other family members to consider.

Here is how the transferred assets would line up.

non-countable	countable	inaccessible
none	none	all cash given away to daughter

This example is used to show the dangers of holding assets jointly and how one sister can help the other protect assets.

NAME:	Ethel and Coretta Johnson
AGES:	81 and 77, respectively
ASSETS:	CDs $10,000
	savings $30,000
	two-family house $150,000
	(all above held jointly)
	insurance, whole life, cash surrender value $10,000
INCOME:	Ethel's social security $350/month
	Coretta's social security $300/month
	joint, from investments $250/month
HEALTH:	Ethel has been in poor health for years and
	has a history of heart problems
	Coretta is in good health

The goal is to protect countable assets from being spent on Ethel's nursing home confinement.

Here's how the assets line up.

non-countable	countable	inaccessible
2-family home	$10,000 CDs $30,000 savings whole life policy, CSV $10,000	none presently

When Siblings Have Time to Plan

If assets remain in the countable column, they will have to be spent on nursing home care before Ethel qualifies for financial assistance (see page 22). If they are transferred to the inaccessible column within 30 months of going into a nursing home, it is presumed that Ethel was trying to hide the assets. (For more on this see pages 80-86.)

Let's look at the various options we might use to protect those assets if there will be 30 months or more before nursing home confinement.

Remember: assets may be protected by:

Option 1   Giving them away

Option 2   Holding them in trust

Option 3   Holding them in certain types of joint accounts

Option 4   An involuntary situation where the applicant is too sick to gain access to countable assets (not applicable in the Johnson's situation)

After examining each option, we will see which is best suited for this specific situation.

Option 1   Giving away assets

Since the investments are held jointly with her sister, Ethel can simply take off her name and social security number. If the investments were in her name alone, they could be transferred to an account with only her sister's name and social security number.

Since Ethel's insurance policy has a cash surrender value of $10,000 and it would have to be spent to zero before eligibility, she should transfer ownership to her sister. She would remain the insured and her sister would continue to be the beneficiary.

If Ethel can stay out of a nursing home for 30 months or more, the money and policy are protected because she is only prohibited from receiving Medicaid if she transfers the assets within 30 months of entering the nursing home.

Drawback

Coretta may die while holding her sister's money and life insurance policy. This can be handled by having her make a will setting up a trust for her sister's benefit. Of course, Coretta would have to choose a person to handle the trust (a trustee) and a person(s) who would get the money upon Ethel's death.

Option 2 Holding assets in trust

There are different kinds of trusts to consider here. For a complete explanation, before continuing go back and read page 25.

Example: An irrevocable trust that *doesn't* protect assets

Ethel sets up The Ethel Johnson Trust naming her sister as trustee and herself as beneficiary. She gives the trustee the power to give her all, some or none of the principal and income. Since she gave discretion over the assets and income to the trustee, Medicaid assumes that the trustee will use her power and make the assets and income available to her sister. In other words, the assets are considered countable and therefore available (see page 22).

Example: An irrevocable trust that *does* protect assets:

Ethel sets up The Ethel Johnson Trust with the same trustee and beneficiary. This time, however, she doesn't give any power to the trustee to give her the assets, only the power to hold them in trust while they generate income for her. The day Ethel goes into the nursing home is the day the snapshot is taken of her assets. However, this time the assets in the trust are not available because the trustee has no authority to give them to her sister.

Here's what Ethel could do:

Plan A Establish an irrevocable trust like the second example above; OR

Plan B Establish a revocable trust naming herself as beneficiary but specifying that the trust becomes irrevocable if she goes into a nursing home or has a long-term illness.

Which plan is best?

Plan A means that Ethel gives up full control of the assets well before she goes into the home. This is the same as giving assets away.

Plan B means that Ethel's assets are countable for 30 months because revocable trusts don't protect countable assets. The trust in Plan B only becomes irrevocable when there's a long-term illness or nursing home confinement. Therefore 30 months must expire before the assets are protected. This option is useful only for people with a great deal of money who can easily afford to pay privately for 30 months. Ethel can't.

If any trust is to be used, Plan A is the best choice because Ethel has a close and trusting relationship with her sister.

Option 3 Holding assets in joint accounts

As we see in our chart, Ethel and Coretta hold their assets jointly in an "or" account. Most joint accounts are held in such a way that either co-holder can get access to the money. This is the case here. Either Ethel *or* Coretta can gain access to the account without the other's signature. Medicaid considers this type of account completely owned by Ethel unless she can prove otherwise. Why? Because presumption in most states is that jointly held funds belong entirely to the person going into the nursing home (see page 86).

There's another type of account that Ethel could open that requires both signatures. This is called an "and" account because both hers *and* her sister's signature are required for either one to get the money.

In most states, an "and" account is protected from being spent on a nursing home if the co-holder refuses to co-sign the check or withdrawal slip to give the ill person access to the account. It remains inaccessible until the person in the nursing home dies.

In our example, if any of Ethel's investments require two signatures, Coretta could make the entire amount inaccessible by simply refusing to co-sign the withdrawal slip. Because regulations vary from state to state, be sure to check with your local welfare office to be sure an "and" account is considered inaccessible in your locale.

Drawbacks

1) As stated above, if either Ethel or Coretta can get access to the funds, Medicaid will consider them entirely owned by Ethel and they will be considered a countable asset.

2) Money held in an "and" account becomes vulnerable in two situations: First, the money becomes a countable asset to Ethel if Coretta dies before her sister. Second, even though Coretta will probably outlive her sister, their money is frozen until her sister dies.

Which of our options is best?

1) Giving away assets

2) Holding assets in trusts

3) Holding assets jointly

Option 1, giving away assets, is the best approach since the sisters have a close relationship and there are no other family members to consider.

Here is how the transferred assets line up.

non-countable	countable	inaccessible
2-family home	none	all cash held by Corretta whole life owned by Corretta on her sister's life

Nieces/Nephews and Aunts/Uncles

Protecting assets for these individuals can be accomplished using the same methods discussed in examples 3 (offspring and single parent, see page 64) and 4 (siblings, see page 71.)

Grandparents and Grandchildren

Protecting assets for these individuals can be accomplished using the same methods discussed in examples 3 (offspring and a single parent, see page 64) and 4 (siblings, see page 71.)

Unrelated People

Protecting assets for the unrelated individuals can be accomplished using the same methods discussed in example 4 (siblings, see page 71.)

5

WHAT TO DO WHEN YOU DON'T HAVE TIME TO PROTECT YOUR ASSETS

There IS Something You Can Do!

The whole concept of planning hinges on understanding the disqualification period. Protecting assets even if you don't have time to plan can be accomplished if you grasp the following statement:

If someone makes a transfer of countable assets for less than fair market value within 30 months of going into a medical institution or nursing home, it is presumed that the transfer was made to hide the assets. Therefore, the person will be disqualified from receiving Medicaid.

Understanding the Disqualification Rule

The following segments interpret this all-important rule and show you how to use it to your advantage.

"If a person makes a transfer of countable assets for less than fair market value..."

Medicaid disqualifies the person going into a medical institution or nursing home for transferring only countable, *not* non-countable assets (see page 23), within 30 months. With the exception of the house, non-countable assets may be transferred to anyone, at any time, even while applying for financial assistance. In other words, you cannot be disqualified from receiving Medicaid because you transfer non-countable assets.

At first glance, this doesn't appear to be of much help because the only non-countable assets a person can keep are the following:

- A house used as a primary residence (in most states this includes two-and three-family homes)
- An amount of cash (usually $2,000) (see chart page 168)
- A car
- Personal jewelry
- Household effects
- A pre-paid funeral
- A burial account (not to exceed $2,500 in most states)
- Term life (as opposed to whole life) insurance policies which have no cash surrender value.

For more information on what your state considers to be non-countable assets see chart 168.

With the exception of the house (see Chapter 7), the other non-countable assets are usually not significant. Their value is that they can be purchased with countable assets at any time even while applying for Medicaid. In addition, Medicaid allows you to spend countable assets on goods or services as long as they are for fair market value and non-countable.

Fair market value is defined as the going rate for goods or services. Medicaid prohibits the transfer of countable assets for less than fair market value. You can't take assets that would have to be spent on a medical institution or nursing home and get rid of them without receiving something of roughly equal value.

Example: Miguel, single, has $25,000 in a money market account and is going into a nursing home in the near future. If he transfers the money outright to his relatives, he will be disqualified from receiving Medicaid for 30 months.

In most states Miguel would be allowed to purchase a pre-paid funeral, open a burial account (up to a specified amount), purchase household goods, and even pay outstanding or necessary bills like utilities, rent, or mortgage and personal bills such as credit cards.

This means that Miguel's funeral and other expenses will be paid out of his money, not his family's.

Example: Edward and Mary have $50,000 in savings. They didn't have time to plan before Mary went into a nursing home on May 1. Under the law in most states, Edward can only keep one half of the assets. However, Mary is allowed to buy with her $25,000 a number of non-countable assets, as Miguel could in our example above.

Let's take this example one step further. In addition to the assets, Edward and Mary have a house with a $10,000 mortgage remaining on it. In most states, the law allows Mary to pay off the entire mortgage from her funds only.

The benefits are obvious. Not only is Mary able to purchase a funeral and pay other expenses, she is allowed to pay off a major debt from her funds which otherwise would go to the nursing home.

"...within 30 months of going into a medical institution or nursing home..."

Medicaid is suspicious of any transfer of countable assets within 30 months of institutionalization. You now understand that countable assets must be transferred at least 30 months before going into a nursing home or medical institution. But what happens if someone is already institutionalized? Does the 30-month rule still apply? Yes! You will have to pay privately for 30 months, but after that the countable assets are protected. Remember: Never apply for Medicaid until the 30-month qualification period has expired (see page 37).

Example: Andrew, single, has $200,000 in cash. He goes into a nursing home on January 1, 1990. He is allowed to transfer all his funds to anyone even after he has been admitted. Yes, he IS disqualified for 30 months from receiving Medicaid and must pay privately. But that's his maximum exposure—30 months. If it costs $30,000 a year, Andrew will have spent $75,000. He has saved $125,000.

"...it is presumed that the transfer was made to hide the assets."

Medicaid presumes that the transfer of countable assets for less than fair market value within 30 months of going into a chronic care facility or nursing home was made to hide those assets. Any presumption can be rebutted. In most states (make sure you check with your Department of Public Welfare), if you can show that at the time the transfer was made there was a legitimate reason for the transfer, those assets are protected and do not have to be spent as countable assets.

Here is a list of what most states consider to be legitimate transfers:

1) At the time countable assets were given away, you were in good health with no medical history of the illness(es) that put you in a nursing home.

2) You had established a pattern of making transfers or gifts, such as reducing the size of your estate for tax purposes, or helping your grandchildren pay for college.

3) At the time you made the transfer or gift, you retained enough countable assets to pay for your then-anticipated medical expenses.

4) At the time you made the transfer or gifts, you were not, nor was your family, aware of the Medicaid regulations on transfer of assets.

Example: Roger, a divorced father of two college-age children, has a savings account of $50,000. For the past three years, he has contributed $2,000 to each child for college expenses. He has no record of major health problems.

Roger suffers a stroke which necessitates nursing home care. He is allowed to take the balance of his savings account ($44,000) and buy non-countable assets (see page 23). If his offspring can prove any one or all of the above criteria, they will not have to give the tuition money back to their father to be spent as a countable asset and Roger will qualify for financial assistance.

These criteria apply to anyone, single or married, who makes a gift or transfers countable assets within 30 months of going into a nursing home.

A note about gift taxes

Federal gift tax applies only if the person giving assets away has more than $600,000 in assets. In other words, you can give away more than $10,000 a year without paying a gift tax. Most states do not have a gift tax but be sure to check with your state Department of Revenue.

How Are You Holding Your Assets? The "AND" Word

Most people hold their assets with someone else. These "or" accounts are set up in such a way that either one *or* the other co-holder can get the money without the permission of the other. However, there are certain types of investments that require two or more signatures to get access. These are called "and" accounts.

Under the law in most states, (make sure you check with your Department of Welfare) all "or" accounts held by husband or wife are joint assets subject to division (see page 29). Worse still, if you hold your investments with anyone other than your husband or wife, they are presumed to be 100 percent the property of the person going into the medical institution or nursing home.

"And" accounts are given special protection. In most states (make sure you check with your Department of

Welfare) the account becomes inaccessible or unavailable (see page 24) to the person going into the nursing home if the co-holder refuses to give permission (in the form of a signature) to get access to the funds. They remain inaccessible until the death of either co-holder.

There are two drawbacks to "and" accounts:

First, if the co-holder dies before the person in the nursing home, the money becomes a countable asset to the patient. He will then be disqualified from receiving assistance until it is spent down.

Second, the money is frozen until the person in the nursing home dies since the co-holder can't get access without the patient's signature. Money taken at any time could well be considered the patient's and therefore a countable asset.

Special Cases

If you are holding your assets jointly with someone, there are a number of ways your account might be set up. The following is a list of commonly used titles on investments:

1) A in trust for B
2) A payable on death (POD) to B
3) A or B as tenants in common
4) A and B as joint tenants with right of survivorship (JTWROS)

In numbers 1 and 2, A (typically a parent, grandparent or sibling) owns 100% of the account, not B. If B goes into the nursing home, the money usually is not considered his.

In number 3, the money usually belongs to the person who goes into the nursing home first, regardless of whose name is first.

Number 4 is considered an "and" account.

There are serious dangers in holding assets with a friend or a sibling. If he is institutionalized before you, Medicaid will presume that the assets belong entirely to him. The key word here is *presume*. In a crisis, most states (make sure to check with your Department of Public Welfare) allow the co-holder to show that he either owns the assets or made a contribution to them in some proportion.

Evidence that can be presented includes a social security number on an account and records of deposits and withdrawals. Also helpful would be to show that the Medicaid applicant's signature was only on the account for convenience, as indicated through documents such as letters. In other words, if it's your money but the co-holder is institutionalized, you would be allowed to keep the money if you could show through evidence that in fact some or all of the money is yours.

You are well advised to look closely at how you are holding accounts, especially if you are single or widowed. Single parents tend to hold their money either with their children or siblings. If money is held with your children, it is considered 100% yours. If with your sibling, the money is considered 100% owned by the person who goes in first unless you can prove it's yours.

This can cause difficulties. For example, if these funds were in a CD that had been rolled over for years, there's no way of proving what funds are yours since there are no deposits or withdrawals.

Spousal Transfers Within the Disqualification Period

Medicaid gives a certain degree of protection to assets held by husbands and wives. The Spousal Impoverishment Act of 1988 (SIA) considers all countable assets, regardless of whose name they are in, to be jointly held and available for division on the day the spouse goes into a medical institution or nursing home. For a further explanation see page 29.

Medicaid allows unlimited transfers of countable assets between husband and wife at any time even if the transfer takes place within 30 months of a spouse's institutionalization. However, if the spouse who receives the assets transfers them to a third party, such as a child, within 30 months, the ill spouse will be disqualified for Medicaid benefits (see pages 43-44).

Example: Gunther and his wife Anna have total countable assets of $50,000. Of this, $40,000 is held in Gunther's IRA account which is in his name only. Gunther is allowed to transfer his IRA to his wife even within 30 months of his going into a nursing home. Anna, however, cannot turn around and give that money to her children without causing Gunther to lose Medicaid benefits.

Medicaid's goal in prohibiting Anna from transferring assets is to have them available for division (see page 29) the day her husband is institutionalized. There is an alternative, however, to having one half or more of these assets spent on Gunther's care. Let's say that Anna, who now has all the money in her name only, refuses to give one half to the nursing home for her husband's care.

There's a technicality that applies in a case like this that has to do with spouses' rights in divorce situations. Although no divorce is contemplated here, Gunther and Anna each would have certain rights to marital assets in the event of a divorce.

All states divide marital assets based on a number of

factors. By law, Gunther can give his rights to marital assets to Medicaid. This is called an assignment of rights. If he does, Medicaid must qualify him for benefits immediately.

Medicaid now has the right to sue Anna for marital assets. Remember, we're not suggesting that Anna file for divorce. Nor are we suggesting that Medicaid will make her divorce her husband. Medicaid simply has the right to go to court to collect whatever assets Gunther might have been entitled to in the hypothetical event of a divorce.

So what's the purpose of this legal maneuver?

Most states have special courts that deal with divorce. Medicaid can only sue in those courts. It is likely that the court would give Anna a more generous division of assets than Medicaid regulations would allow. In considering this option, you must weigh the expense of attorney's fees against the additional monies you might receive from the court beyond what Medicaid already allows.

Note: If Gunther is totally incapacitated, Medicaid will pay for him if his doctor writes a report stating that he is too ill to perform the necessary actions to get to his assets.

Example: Gunther and Anna have countable assets of $150,000. Under the Spousal Impoverishment Act she is allowed to keep only $60,000. Most states will usually divide assets equally in a divorce. There is an excellent chance Anna would be allowed to keep at least $75,000 if Medicaid sued her in probate court.

Appealing Medicaid Decisions on Asset Division

This option is available only to spouses. As we discussed earlier, a non-institutionalized spouse is allowed to keep an amount of money when the husband or wife goes into a chronic care facility or nursing home. This can range from a low of $12,000 to a maximum of $60,000 depending upon state regulations (see pages 29-31). The Spousal Impoverishment Act does allow for an appeal process. Each state has an appeal system for spouses who feel that the money they have left after asset division will not generate enough income to live on. If you believe that the assets left to the stay-at-home spouse are not sufficient to generate income, you can ask for an appeals hearing through your local Department of Public Welfare.

Insult to Injury — Suing Your Spouse for Divorce

Under the Spousal Impoverishment Act (SIA), the maximum a stay-at-home spouse is allowed to keep from joint assets is $60,000. Couples with more than $120,000 in assets may want to consider the possibility of divorce proceedings.

This option, like the above, applies only to spouses. SIA provides that a court may make a division of assets that may be more favorable than Medicaid allows.

Example: Evan and Lillian have joint countable assets of $150,000 on the day Lillian goes into a nursing home. Under SIA, all Evan could keep is one half of the total assets or $60,000, whichever is less. However, if Evan were to file a divorce petition, it is likely he would get at least half of their joint property and maybe more, depending upon his financial circumstances.

Example: George is married with two children. While watching television one day, he collapses. He is rushed to the hospital and diagnosed as having had a severe stroke. His prognosis: He will be in a coma for the rest of his life. George is 46 years old. The family's total assets — an $80,000 IRA.

Under Medicaid regulations, all George's wife could keep of countable assets is one half of her husband's IRA worth $80,000. By filing an action for divorce she could request from the court more than $40,000 based on her limited earning capacity and the needs of two minor children.

Filing for divorce usually should not be considered unless you have first filed and lost an appeal to the Department of Public Welfare. This is a complicated procedure that should only be done with the assistance of a lawyer.

Protecting Assets by Claiming Disability

In Chapter 3, we discussed a group of assets which Medicaid could not reach because the person going into the nursing home couldn't reach them. These are called inaccessible assets. In most states (make sure you check with your Department of Public Welfare), monies can be protected if you can show that the person applying for Medicaid cannot get access to them because he or she is too sick. The investments remain frozen until the person dies.

Example: Eduardo is single and on life support systems. He has $50,000 in his name alone which would be countable and therefore spent on a nursing home. If someone can present evidence to Medicaid that Eduardo cannot gain access because of his condition, the money remains intact and he would qualify for Medicaid immediately. Medicaid may require that a guardian or conservator be appointed (see pages 146-148) to gain access to Eduardo's accounts. Even if Medicaid did not force the issue they could put a lien on the estate after he died.

6

PROTECTING INCOME FROM MEDICAID

Most of an unmarried person's income cannot be protected from a nursing home or other long-term care institution. There are three exceptions: He may keep 1) a small personal needs account, and 2) premiums for health care coverage such as Medex. 3) A home allowance in most states if he can show he will be coming home (see chart page 163). However, Medicaid makes a provision for married couples that allows the stay-at-home spouse to keep a minimum of combined income.

Spousal Impoverishment Act Guidelines

As of October 1, 1989, under the Spousal Impoverishment Act, a non-institutionalized spouse may be allowed to keep a certain amount of his or her spouse's earned income. Income is defined as any money received from investments, pensions, social security, trusts, royalties, etc. received by either party. The minimum amount the states allow the stay-at-home spouse to keep is $815 per month; the maximum is $1,500 monthly plus certain additional allowances (these amounts will increase automatically each year). The stay-at-home spouse may be entitled to additional monies if she can show that housing and utility expenses exceed 30% of the monthly amount the state allows her to keep (see page 98).

Example: Louis and Mae are married with a total income of

$2,200 a month, broken down as follows:

Louis has $800 in social security and a pension of $1,200.

Mae has $200 in social security.

If their state allowed Mae to keep only the minimum of $815, she would be able to keep $615 of her husband's income in addition to her $200. The rest would go to the nursing home with the exception of a small personal needs account for him and a deduction for his Medex payment.

If their state allowed Mae to keep $1,300 a month she would then be allowed to keep $1,100 of his income in addition to her $200.

Note: The state allows a stay-at-home spouse to keep all her income including that earned from working and income from the assets she is allowed to keep. If Mae has monthly income from a part-time job of $1500, she does not have to give money to her husband; she just would not be able to get any of his income. In addition, Medicaid usually divides investment income in half. Our example uses a wife as a stay-at-home spouse, but the rules apply just the same if the husband is at home.

Other Ways to Secure More Income

Spouses who cannot survive financially on the allowance given to them by Medicaid can appeal directly to the state's welfare office. You must show that the income available is not sufficient to cover your needs because of extraordinary expenses or unusual circumstances. Be prepared to document your request.

Finally, SIA does allow the stay-at-home spouse to file a petition in the family or probate court that handles domestic relations to secure more income than Medicaid would allow.

The stay-at-home spouse may be entitled to additional monies (a shelter allowance) if she can show that the monthly maintenance allowance ($815) is insufficient to keep up her house. There is a formula that Medicaid uses to figure out the maximum additional allowance. The figuring is complicated and best explained by an example.

Walter is in a nursing home and has qualified for Medicaid. His monthly income is $1,200. His wife Nora continues to live at home. Her income is $450 from social security. The mortgage on the house is $600 per month and the utitlities are $100 monthly.

Here are the steps that Nora should take to determine if she can get more than $815 a month.

1. Add the monthly amount that Nora pays for her mortgage ($600) and utilities ($100), for a total of $700.
2. Take 30% of $815, Nora's standard monthly maintenance allowance. That amount is $244.
3. Deduct $244 from the total amount Nora pays for her mortgage and utilities ($700.) $700 minus $244 equals $456, called her excess shelter allowance.

4. Add $815 and $456 = $1,271.
5. Deduct Nora's monthly income ($450) from $1,271.
6. The figure arrived at in step 5 is Nora's new monthly maintenance allowance.

$815.00	Nora's standard monthly maintenance allowance
+ 456.00	excess shelter allowance, see 2 and 3 above
1271.00	
- 450.00	Nora's monthly income from social security
$821.00	Nora's new monthly maintenance allowance

The question the stay-at-home spouse must ask is: Does she think that her monthly housing expenses eat up too much of her monthly maintenance allowance? Always assume that they do and use the above formula to see if you may be entitled to more than the minimum. In Nora's case, she can only get $6.00 more under this formula.

Remember: The only unquestioned increase that Medicaid allows in the monthly maintenance amount is to cover mortgage, rent and utilities.

PROTECTING THE HOUSE — A VERY SPECIAL ASSET

Who Can and Who Can't Transfer a Home

Does owning your house jointly avoid a Medicaid lien?

Prior to July 1, 1988, states had different interpretations of Medicaid regulations. Since Medicaid is funded 50% by the states and 50% by the federal government, each state felt free to adopt rules that suited its particular circumstances. As a result, there was little uniformity.

Although the states agree on little, everyone seems to support the notion that a person's home is a very special asset that should be given certain protections that ordinary assets don't have. Most states allow the primary residence to remain a non-countable asset (see chart pages 168-171) even if no one lives there. Many states even allow the house to be transferred to family members or anyone else, not only within 30 months of requesting Medicaid, but even if the person making the transfer is on Medicaid!

But wait for a moment. Is it fair to allow a Medicaid recipient to transfer the house solely for the purpose of avoiding repayment for money paid on their behalf? Put another way, should the taxpayer be subsidizing inheritances? Most of us would answer a resounding "No"— with one exception: If the house being transferred belongs to *our* family member or friend.

Congress realized that the states did not have the political backbone to prohibit these transfers. If any state representative voted to place a lien on a voter's property he wouldn't have a prayer of getting re-elected.

As of July 1, 1988, Congress mandated that the states adopt, within approximately a year and a half, the following rules regarding the transfer of a house:

For single persons A transfer of the house to anyone within 30 months of institutionalization or applying for Medicaid triggers a disqualification from Medicaid until either 30 months passes or the nursing home bills accumulate to the value of the house.

Example: Lee has a house worth $65,000. She transfers it to her sister for one dollar on January 1, 1990. She goes into a nursing home on January 1, 1991. The nursing home charges $30,000 a year or $75,000 for 30 months. Since she transferred the house within 30 months, she will not be eligible for Medicaid until either July 1, 1992 (30 months from January 1, 1990) or if/when her nursing home bills reach the value of her home ($65,000) In this example, Lee will qualify for Medicaid prior to July 1, 1992 because the nursing home bill for 30 months exceeds the value of the house. She can request assistance once the bill reaches $65,000.

For married couples Either spouse is allowed to transfer without penalty his or her interest in their home to the other spouse at any time, even while on Medicaid. However, the spouse who becomes sole owner of the home *may not* be able to transfer it to another party. (This question is unresolved at the moment so you must check with an attorney.) To do so might trigger the 30 month disqualification rule for the institutionalized spouse.

However, if the institutionalized spouse dies, the surviving spouse is free to transfer the property without penalty. In other words, even though Medicaid paid, the house cannot be used for reimbursement.

Example: Jerry and Bess are married and own a house jointly. Bess goes into a nursing home on June 1, 1990. She is allowed to sign over her interest to her husband even though she may request Medicaid within 30 months. Jerry may not be able to transfer the property while his wife is alive. After she passes away, however, he is free to transfer the house without a lien.

1) If Bess dies having been on Medicaid, and Jerry dies with the property in his name, Medicaid will put a lien on it.

2) If Jerry dies before Bess, and doesn't change his will (which like most husbands leaves everything to the wife), the

property immediately goes to her and is subject to a lien at her death.

Exceptions to the rule

Medicaid allows certain exceptions to the above prohibition against transferring houses. A single person or married couple can transfer a home to

1) a child who is blind, disabled or under 21.

2) a sibling who owns a share of the home and has resided there for at least one year before the co-holder goes into the nursing home.

3) a child (of any age) who has resided in the home for at least two years before the parent's institutionalization and can show that he has cared for the parent at home.

4) anyone at any time as long as it is for fair market value.

5) anyone, providing the purpose of the transfer is not to qualify for Medicaid. For example, a person gives his house to his children while healthy for the purpose of avoiding probate or estate taxes. Later he is permanently disabled in an accident and is forced to go into a nursing home within 30 months of making the transfer. This transfer would probably not disqualify him for Medicaid.

One last possibility — Even though the transfer of a house would ordinarily disqualify a person for Medicaid, he may still receive benefits if he can show that he would suffer undue hardship by not being granted benefits. This alternative is very unusual and is rarely accepted by Medicaid.

Protecting the House—When There's Time To Plan

There are four options for protecting your home if you have 30 months or more to plan. They are:

> Give away the house
>
> Give away the house with a life estate
>
> Put the house in trust
>
> Hold the house jointly

Giving Away the House

A person is free to give a house to whomever he chooses and later qualify for Medicaid providing the transfer takes place at least 30 months prior to institutionalization or application for Medicaid. There are three considerations before you do this.

First, giving your home away leaves you with no control. There are more than a few cases of a daughter who has tried to have parents evicted from their home or a son who has lost the house through bad investments or a divorce.

Second, while you may trust the person or persons to whom you give your house, you sacrifice the one-time $125,000 exemption from capital gains taxes (assuming you are over 55) if you later decide to sell the house.

Third, by giving away your home, you pass on to the receiver a greater capital gains tax liability when the house is sold. Capital gains is the difference between the basis (what you paid for the house plus what you spent on major improvements) and the sale price. Most older Americans paid relatively little for their homes and have seen their homes appreciate greatly in value. They have a low basis relative to the value of the house, which means higher taxes. This basis is passed on to the recipient of the house. When she later sells the property at fair market value, she pays a substantial tax on the capital gains.

Giving Away the House with a Life Estate

When a person gives away his house he may make a provision that he keep an interest in the property for the remainder of his life. That interest may take the form of a life estate through which he has a lifelong right to live in the home as well as to receive any income or benefits that may accrue from the property.

A life estate does not mean that you *own* the property; it means that you have an *interest* that ends when you die. Medicaid can only place a lien on your property to recoup nursing home expenses if you alone legally own the property when you die. Assuming that you absolutely, positively are willing to stake your life on the integrity of the person you want to hold your house, a life estate is a very good way to protect your house from a Medicaid lien.

In addition, there are significant tax advantages. You may be able to claim a portion or all of the capital gains exemption if the property is sold during your life. The recipient also avoids the problems we discuss above when the house is eventually sold. See your accountant for a complete explanation of the tax savings.

Putting the House in Trust

For an explanation of different kinds of trusts, please read pages 25-28. In that chapter, we see that revocable trusts can't be used to protect *countable* assets. But remember, your house is a *non-countable* asset (see page 23). Therefore, placing it in a revocable trust (even though it's an instrument you fully control) does not in most states jeopardize Medicaid eligibility.

In most states, liens are not placed on the Medicaid recipient's home until he dies and then only if the property is in his name only. A home placed in a revocable trust is owned by the trust, not the Medicaid recipient. It stands to reason that if there's nothing in the recipient's name no lien can be attached. (Be sure to check with an attorney to see how your state treats revocable trusts.)

The advantages of a revocable trust are that it

1) gives the trustee absolute control over the property during his lifetime.

2) does away with the need for a co-owner of the property.

3) gives the person who set up the trust (if over age 55) the entire $125,000 capital gains exemption if the property is sold during his life.

4) avoids probate.

5) minimizes capital gains.

Note: In some states legislators are considering placing liens on homes when the applicant first goes into a nursing home. Therefore, although the house can be transferred, the lien goes with it. When the house is sold, Medicaid would get reimbursed. Be sure to check with your Department of Public Welfare to find out what regulations apply in your state.

Holding the House Jointly

A single or widowed person may consider holding his house jointly with the person who will eventually inherit it. However, joint ownership is both impractical and dangerous. Impractical, because you no longer have full control over the property. Dangerous, because the co-holder may go into a nursing home before you do.

For example, if Medicaid does not consider the house the primary residence of the institutionalized co-holder, it would have to be sold and one half the proceeds spent on his nursing home bills.

Another problem—You may decide to sell the house. Co-holding costs you at least one half of the capital gains exemption (assuming you are over 55).

Other problems—What if your co-holder gets a divorce and the house is considered part of the couple's common property? Or your co-holder may get sued.

If you must hold property jointly, make sure you do so with a younger person such as your son or daughter, and insist that he or she enter into an agreement with the spouse that exempts the property from their joint marital assets.

Does Holding the House Jointly Avoid a Lien?

In most states, joint ownership of real estate avoids a Medicaid lien since a lien attaches only to property that is owned individually. The two most common forms of co-ownership are joint tenancy (Steve Smith *and* Carl Jones) and tenants in common (Steve Smith *or* Carl Jones).

Joint tenancy means that if Steve dies, Carl automatically gets his share of the property and vice versa.

Tenants in common means that if Steve dies, his heirs get his share automatically, not Carl; and if Carl dies, his heirs automatically get his share of the property, not Steve.

Property held in joint tenancy in most states is protected from a lien because the share belonging to the deceased co-owner never goes through his estate. Instead, it goes automatically to the surviving co-holder. Not so with tenants in common. The share belonging to the deceased co-holder goes through his estate, which immediately makes it available for a lien.

If you are single, as a way of avoiding a Medicaid lien, you may choose to hold your home in a joint tenancy with someone else.

Warning: States have varying regulations covering this issue. Your state may not agree with the above interpretation. They may hold that a lien attaches to the deceased's one half share even though it doesn't go through probate. Be sure to check with an attorney or your local welfare office.

Panic—There's No Time to Plan

No time to plan means that a person will be going into a medical institution or nursing home or requesting Medicaid assistance within 30 months of transferring his home.

Married couples There's no problem here since the law allows the person going into the nursing home to transfer his interest to the spouse even while on Medicaid. Under present regulations, the spouse who now has the house in her name can give it away or sell it while her husband is alive or after his death without penalty.

Single people Transferring your house within 30 months of going into a nursing home poses a difficult situation for single people. Your best option is to see if you fall into any of the exceptions mentioned on page 105. If you don't, here's a grim option:

Don't try to transfer the house at all if it is worth a great deal of money (say, over $200,000). Medicaid *will* place a lien on it when you die. But since Medicaid usually pays only half of the private daily rate, the bite out of your estate will be less than if you pay privately for institutionalization.

For example, if a nursing home charges private pay patients $100 a day, the rate that Medicaid pays for the same person is about $50. Upon your death your family will have to pay the lien, but it's only half of what the private rate would have been.

The only problem is that your state may have adopted the federal regulation which mandates that a primary residence be sold after six months of institutionalization if the patient cannot show that he will be returning home. Check with your local Department of Public Welfare.

Example: Tom is divorced with three children. His only asset is his house, which is worth $200,000. On January 1, 1991, he will need nursing home care. Cost, $3,000 per month. He transfers his house to his children on June 1, 1990. Tom will be disqualified from receiving Medicaid benefits either for 24 months or until the cost of the nursing home equals the value of his house ($200,000.) Either way Tom has to sell his home to come up with $72,000 (24 months x $3,000.) Add to this the capital gains tax, and his children will receive very little when they are forced to sell the house. However, this is the family's maximum exposure ($72,000 plus capital gains tax).

What if Tom keeps the property in his name? Sure, there's a lien on the house upon his death, but Medicaid is running up a bill at only one half the rate that Tom would be running up as a private patient. As long as Tom does not stay in a nursing home for a long period of time this option will save money.

However, if his stay extends for more than four years, this option becomes more costly than simply selling the house. Why? Because, four years of nursing home care at a Medicaid reimbursed rate of $50 a day ($18,250 a year) would equal $72,000, the maximum exposure (excluding taxes) in the first example. Therefore, after four years, this option provides no savings.

THE INSURANCE DILEMMA

THE INSURANCE DILEMMA

Until recently, few people understood that Medicare and all other forms of health insurance do not pay for custodial care in a nursing home. Because of recent media exposure given to the subject of catastrophic illness, more people have begun to face the seriousness of the problem. When an illness strikes that requires long-term custodial care, there are only three alternatives to pay: cash, Medicaid and nursing home insurance.

Nursing home insurance pays a certain amount per day for a set number of months of custodial care. There is a desperate need for such policies. Unfortunately, the truth is that finding a good policy is very difficult at this time.

Medigap policies

Insurance companies spend millions of dollars annually advertising the virtues of policies that take up where Medicare leaves off. With names like Medigap and Secure Care 65, these pitches lull older Americans into a false sense of security. Many people believe these policies will cover nursing home care. It's an expensive mistake. None of these plans covers custodial care in nursing homes. Quite frankly, they don't cover much of anything. At best, they may supplement and pay some of the deductibles. (A report on abuses in the sale of Medigap insurance and what the states are doing about them is available FREE from the Office of Public Affairs, Health Care Financing Administration, Room 435-H, 200 Independence Ave., Washington, D.C. 20201.)

When you are considering insurance, the thing you must understand is this: If you want coverage for a nursing home, you have to buy a *nursing home policy*.

Long-Term Care Insurance

The insurance industry has been quick to recognize that as people live longer the likelihood increases that they will end up in nursing homes for some period of time. In the last few years, over 70 insurance companies have come up with long term care policies.

Unfortunately, most of them aren't worth the paper they're written on. They are so full of restrictions, exceptions and limitations that one recent survey conducted by Congress found that less than a third of policies ever pay a dime! But that doesn't mean that nursing home insurance is a bad idea. In fact, in certain cases, it may make some sense.

Assuming you find the right policy, and that's a big assumption, nursing home insurance is primarily useful for one thing—maintaining control over your assets until you need nursing home care. This book has presented a number of ways you can protect assets in the event of a long-term nursing home stay if you have time to plan. Every option, in one form or another, involves giving up control at least 30 months before going into a nursing home.

This gives rise to a dilemma: The best time to protect your life savings is when you're healthy. However, to do it you generally have to give away your assets and relinquish control. Let's say you decide it's worth it and strip away all your assets. But suppose you never need a nursing home—you die peacefully in your own bed twenty years later. For two decades, you live with the discomfort of not being in control of your finances. Not an easy decision to live with.

Here's another idea: A nursing home insurance policy can buy you time. Here's how: It allows you to maintain control of your countable assets until you need a nursing home, and, in some cases, permits you to transfer those assets with less economic consequence to you. You are covered, partially or fully, by the policy for the 30 month disqualification period during which you do not receive Medicaid.

Note: If you are considering a nursing home policy, you must plan how the assets would be taken out of your name if you were institutionalized and too incapacitated to move them yourself. The 30 month period only starts to run when assets are removed from your name. This problem can be overcome in two ways—hold your assets jointly or put together a power of attorney (see page 148).

Example: Noreen is 65 years old and widowed. She has two children. She has a house and $135,000 in cash and securities. She has two options to protect her assets from a nursing home: While she's still healthy, she can give away her assets in any number of ways (see pages 64-70). If at least 30 months go by between the date of transfer and the date of confinement, the assets are protected. However, since she's healthy, years will probably pass before she needs a nursing home — if ever.

Or she can buy a nursing home insurance policy.

Like most people, Noreen wants to keep her financial independence. She doesn't want to worry about what the answer might be if she goes to her kids and asks for her money. She doesn't want to worry about her kids getting sued or divorced and thereby jeopardizing the assets. In short, she wants control.

To keep control, she purchases a policy that pays, for example, $100 a day for custodial care in a nursing home for three years. She has a stroke in five years. She can now transfer her assets *to her children or whomever she wants, even on or after the day she goes into the home.*

Although the transfer disqualifies Noreen from receiving Medicaid benefits for 30 months, the policy steps in and pays the first $100 per day for that disqualification period. If Noreen did not have this policy, she might have lost all or most of her assets and a lien might have been put on her house when she died.

A good policy for a person in reasonably good health, at age 65, averages between $1,200 and $2,000 a year. That is high but the alternatives of giving away your assets or placing them in an irrevocable trust to protect them will cost you too. Give away assets and you give away control. Whether it's outright or in an irrevocable trust, you're always going to have to go to someone and ask permission to get your money.

Giving away assets can be an expensive proposition as well. Most retired people are in a lower federal tax bracket (15%) than their children (28%.) If your offspring hold your assets, you pay a 13% penalty yearly. For example $100,000 generates about $8,000 a year in interest. The tax on those earnings, in a 15% bracket, is about $1,200. If your children are in a 28% bracket the tax would almost double.

Even if you can accept the additional tax, you will find it difficult to live with this: Nursing homes avoid taking welfare patients even though its illegal to do so. Most likely, you would have to come up with at least six to nine months of private funds to get into a first class facility near your family. That means the people who hold your money have to turn over a good chunk of it to "grease the skids" to get you in.

How much for six to nine months? In 10 years, figure in the neighborhood of $50,000 to $75,000. Nice neighborhood. Add to that the tax penalty you've paid over the years.

On the other hand, let's say that you pay $2,000 a year for a policy for 10 years. At first glance, this seems like a great deal of money. But wait. Do the arithmetic. Ten years of premiums at $2,000 per year is $20,000. That's a lot better than $50,000 to $75,000 plus taxes. And the policy usually pays for at least 36 months, assuring you of a bed in a nursing home.

The benefits are appealing. The problem is that a recent report issued by the Families USA Foundation found that only about 15 percent of the elderly population can afford even a minimal policy that provides only partial coverage, let alone one like the above costing $2,000 or more annually for relatively extensive coverage. And that price only covers one spouse! For the vast majority of senior citizens, nursing home policies are just too expensive.

If you are one of the minority who are not staggered by the cost of premiums and you want to protect substantial assets, you may decide to look into nursing home insurance. You want to maintain control of your assets. As a responsible person, you don't want to be a burden to your family or society. You're ready to start shopping for coverage. Unfortunately, it's not that simple.

For many reasons, buying nursing home insurance is as confusing and perilous as buying a used car. The problem is that nursing home insurance is a relatively new product and insurance companies are struggling to figure out what kinds of coverage they can make a profit on. To cover themselves, they offer policies that are worded in such a way that the insurer has a back door out of paying you the coverage you thought you were buying.

NURSING HOME INSURANCE — Confusion and Deception

Is this deliberate deception? Maybe. On top of that, the agent may not know much about what he is selling you, or he may misrepresent the policy in order to make a sale. Like a used car, you may buy a policy that looks good but is actually a lemon and you won't find out till it's too late When it comes time to collect, an ambiguously worded provision may disqualify you from receiving any benefits. When you buy a nursing home insurance policy you may be buying a nightmare.

If you can get past the prohibitive cost, there are many reasons why nursing home insurance may not provide you with the protection you want. One of the most important is inflation.

To understand how inflation affects this kind of insurance, let's look at Massachusetts, a state that has been a pioneer in setting high standards for long-term care insurance.

Of 77 companies now marketing this product, only four currently meet Massachusetts's relatively stringent criteria for licensing. Each company offers coverage in a variety of packages. But it is only the most extensive, and thus *expen*sive of these that offers reasonable protection against the staggering and *rising* cost of long-term care. Here's how that works:

Massachusetts requires that the companies offer an optional inflation rider. That rider is critical. If you don't elect to take it, your coverage will be continually eroded by the rising cost of living. You will have to pay tomorrow's inflated bills with today's devalued dollars.

Unfortunately, even the most generous rider available in Massachusetts lags well behind the actual rate of increase in medical care costs. That means that the policyholder's benefits diminish every year.

Let's say at age 65 you buy a policy that pays $100 a day, for three years of care in a nursing home, with an inflation rider. In ten years you are institutionalized for two and a half years. Your bill at that time will be about $200,000 at the current rate of inflation.

You will receive a net $120,000 in benefits, but you may still have to make up $80,000 out of pocket for a bed in an average (nothing fancy) nursing home.

Ethical issues and logistics aside, nursing home insurance doesn't put you ahead financially of the option of moving your assets, waiting thirty months, "greasing the skids" with cash to the nursing home and applying for Medicaid. What it *has* done is allow you to maintain full control of your assets.

Insurance companies tailor their policies to the regulations in each state. Therefore, this example may not work out the same way in your state. The costs and benefits may be different, but the problems will be the same. Wherever you live, if you buy a policy without inflation protection, your coverage will effectively shrink every year.

One other consideration regarding coverage: Some companies tout their home care coverage as a way for you to use your benefits at home so that you won't need to go into a nursing home. According to Dr. James Firman of United Seniors Health Cooperative, which participated in a study of the home care component of nursing home insurance, "For most people, the home care coverage won't cover much of anything. Don't buy this kind of policy if your purpose is to stay out of a nursing home. There are so many restrictions and technicalities in these policies that there would be only a small fraction of the total home care need that people would be able to collect on."

Restrictions and technicalities are the *other* big problem with nursing home insurance. *Consumer Reports* in May 1988 published an article entitled "Who can afford a nursing home?" This 11-page survey of nursing home insurance stated: "We'd like to report that private insurance policies can meet the increasingly urgent need for long-term-care coverage at a moderate cost. But many of the insurance policies we looked at were very expensive, severely limited in their coverage, or both... People who shop for them will run into a crazy quilt of charges, waivers, and limitations that confuses even insurance agents who sell the policies."

The article goes on to address a whole litany of tricky restrictions. For instance, most policies reviewed by *Consumer Reports* exclude care for mental and nervous disorders. While few actually exclude Alzheimer's disease by name, many policies state that they will only pay for "mental disorders associated with a demonstrable organic disease." Alzheimer's is considered an organic disorder, but *Consumer Reports* points out that only a biopsy or an autopsy can confirm a diagnosis of Alzheimer's. So if you were to develop Alzheimer's, a disorder affecting about half of all nursing home patients, would you be covered? Maybe yes, maybe no. But you wouldn't know till it was too late.

Another hitch: Policies which explicitly cover Alzheimer's frequently will not pay benefits to patients who have not been hospitalized before going into a nursing home. As most Alzheimer's patients do not require hospitalization prior to going into a nursing home, most policyholders with this disorder would be disqualified from receiving benefits under this provision.

The examples above are but two of a long list of confusing, misleading and deceptive practices discussed in *Consumer Reports* May 1988 article.

A storm of public protest has led to some reforms. In an attempt to curtail the worst abuses, the National Association of Insurance Commissioners (NAIC) drafted a model law and regulations that have been adopted in some form by about two-thirds of the states. In some states, many unfair practices have been outlawed and companies not complying are barred from doing business. Other states have adopted weaker versions of the changes.

You can call your state Division of Insurance (see chart page 178) to find out whether your state has adopted some form of the law or regulation. Ask if a summary of the regulation or the regulation itself is available and get the names of those companies that are approved to market long-term care policies in your state. When shopping for insurance, ask the agent to give you a sample policy, not just the promotional brochure *about* the policy. If there is any point on which you are confused by the language of the policy, ask for a clarification in writing.

Although the NAIC reforms are helpful to those who are shopping for a policy, approximately 800,000 people are currently paying for old, potentially useless policies they bought before the regulations went into effect. The regulations are *not* retroactive. If you purchased a policy before your state adopted the new regulations, it's time to review your policy before you pay another dime in premiums. By the way, in states without the new guidelines, many insurance companies are still selling the old, virtually worthless policies.

In October 1989, *Consumer Reports* printed an update entitled "Paying for a Nursing Home," which spotlighted yet another problem presently being scrutinized by the National Association of Insurance Commissioners—the practice of "post-claims underwriting." Many insurance companies make a practice of waiting until you make a claim to determine your fitness for coverage—and it's legal. What that means is this: You might put in a claim as much as two years after you began paying for your policy and be told, "Sorry, you're not eligible because you didn't disclose that condition when we sold you the policy." The condition might have occurred some years ago — before the period you were asked to disclose. Nevertheless, you could still be ineligible. Or, your claim might be refused if you told the agent who sold you the policy about the condition and he neglected to write it down. (He has an incentive to be forgetful about marginal conditions that might disqualify you because he gets a commission on the sale.) Or, you might be denied benefits even if the illness that put you in the nursing home was unrelated to the one you didn't disclose.

There are a number of other disqualifying subtleties insurance companies use to keep you from collecting on your claim. *Consumer Reports'* conclusion: "It's impossible to know in advance how an insurance company will behave when you need to file a claim on a long-term-care policy. Until more claims have been filed, and until insurance regulators make public the records of companies engaging in post-claims underwriting, you must protect yourself."

To do this, you must be scrupulously thorough and honest in answering all questions on the application form. Don't even think about hiding any medical problem, big or small. Double check the application after the agent fills it out to be sure there are no errors or omissions. Any of these might later be used by the company to rescind your coverage.

A company that examines your medical history and requires an attending physician's statement before issuing the policy may be less likely to practice post-claims underwriting. Companies that issue a policy within a very short period of time may be more likely to disqualify your claim later when they take the time to scrutinize your medical history.

Other tips from *Consumer Reports* October, 1989: Protecting Yourself — Rules to Remember.

• Be wary of a company willing to issue a policy to someone over age 85. A company eager to issue coverage to very old people may have less intention of paying the claims that inevitably will follow. Check with your state insurance department to see if it has information on how the company pays claims, especially those made by the very old.

• Avoid policies that require you to be hospitalized before a nursing- home stay and those that require a prior level of care before benefits are payable. Even though the model law written by the National Association of Insurance Commissioners prohibits such restrictions, not all states have adopted the model, and there are still policies sold with these limitations. They could cause you or your family a lot of grief later.

• Carefully read the policy's definitions for levels of care. If the policy says it pays for skilled, intermediate, and custodial care, make sure it pays for them in any type of facility, not just one specializing in skilled-nursing care. If the definitions seem too restrictive, look for another policy. Some policies make no distinction among levels of care. They will pay for any type of care in any licensed facility. It's worth considering these less-restrictive policies to avoid haggling over definitions when the need for care arises.

• Buy one good policy. If you have a policy and want either higher benefits or less-restrictive coverage, ask your present company about upgrading it. Upgrading from your own company may be cheaper than buying a new policy from a *different company and paying the company's expenses, including the agent's commission, all over again. (Some companies offer policyholders a chance to upgrade without rechecking their medical condition. Ask if your company will do this. However, if you have a chronic health condition, you may not be able to switch.)*

If your company won't upgrade your policy by, for example, eliminating the requirements for prior hospitalization or prior levels of care, you should shop for a new company. But keep your old policy until you have received the new one.

• If you own a policy, make sure a friend, family member, or your doctor knows where it is, when the premiums are due, and how to submit claims to the insurance company.

When you are considering a long-term care policy, you must weigh all the factors that are specific to your own situation. An insurance agent is not an unbiased resource for helping you make a decision.

Before you buy a long-term care policy, you *must* educate yourself. Make a trip to your local library to read the two *Consumer Reports* articles discussed above. Or to order reprints or back issues, write to *Consumer Reports*, Back Issue Department, P.O. Box 53016, Boulder, Colorado, 80322-3016. (See Other Sources of Information, page 133.)

As a general rule, with nursing home insurance you get what you pay for. The best coverage is expensive, $2,000 a year and up. The more affordable policies generally offer only partial protection according to Ron Pollack, of Families USA Foundation. "Even the most expensive of these policies have shortcomings that limit the protection you get. The cheapest have truly worrisome limitations."

Better policies will include provisions for using benefits in other ways, such as an alternative care plan and/or home care. For example, a policy holder and his family are allowed to present a plan of care to the insurance company that permits the individual to stay at home and still receive benefits.

Another thing, before you buy a policy, be sure you can afford to make the payments over a long period of time. This is a form of term insurance; if you cancel, you will receive nothing back.

Group policies tend to be less expensive, however, most are unregulated by the states. Be very careful. Do not buy on price alone.

Excerpts from *Consumer Reports* copyright 1988 by Consumer Union of United States, Inc., Mt. Vernon, NY 10553. Excepted by permission from *Consumer Reports*, May 1988.

Other sources of information

Long-Term Care: A Dollar and Sense Guide
United Seniors Health Cooperative
1334 G Street, Suite 500, Washington, D.C. 20005
64 pages, Cost: $6.95

National Long Term Care Campaign
P.O. Box 27394, Washington, D.C. 20038

ElderLaw News (four-page quarterly newsletter)
10 Winthrop Square, Boston, MA 02110
$15 for a one year subscription

The Medicaid Planning Handbook
Alexander A. Bove, Jr., Esq.
(covers Massachusetts only)
Ormand Sacker Press
P.O. Box 4526, Boston, MA 02101
$23 plus $3.50 p & h

Your local Office of Elder Affairs

Your state Division of Insurance

The following is the Massachusetts long-term care regulation based on the guidelines developed by the National Association of Insurance Commissioners. The Massachusetts version (and that adopted by the state of Washington) go well beyond the NAIC regulation in protecting consumers from insurance company abuses. This regulation will provide you with standards for evaluating any policy you might be considering, particularly important if your state does not exercise control over long-term care insurers.

You may call your state's insurance commissioner to get a copy of the regulations (if any) that apply in your state.

Commonwealth Of Massachusetts

SUMMARY OF SIGNIFICANT PROVISIONS OF 211 CMR 65.00

LONG-TERM CARE INSURANCE REGULATIONS

APPLICABILITY: Regulation applies to non-group (individual) policies issued on or after August 1, 1989.

STANDARD DEFINITIONS: Insurers must use standardized definitions (e.g., medically necessary, skilled nursing care, home health care.) This will help consumers compare policies.

BENEFITS:

(a) Combination nursing home and home health care policy:

Mandatory:

Must offer 730 days or $36,500 of a combined/ interchangeable nursing home and home health care benefit.

Nursing home benefit must cover all three levels in a nursing home for a minimum of $50.00/day.

Home health benefits must be at least 50% of the nursing home benefit.

No policy need pay for care in excess of the actual cost.

Optional:

Policies may offer optional benefits: adult day care, adult foster care, chore care, homemaker, respite care and social day care. Benefits must be of some economic value.

(b) Home health care-only policies:

Mandatory:

Must offer at least 312 days of $18,250 of benefits.

Optional:

Policies may offer optional benefits: adult day care, adult foster care, chore care, homemaker, respite care and social day care. Benefits must be of some economic value.

ELIMINATION PERIOD: Policies may not require an elimination period (deductible) greater than 100 days (home health care and nursing home.)

PRIOR TREATMENT:

Prior hospitalization may NOT be required as a precondition for nursing home benefits.

A level of care in a nursing home may not be conditioned upon any other level of care in a nursing home.

A nursing home stay may not be required as a precondition for home health care benefits.

OTHER BENEFIT PROVISIONS: Benefits must be available 365 days per year unless the maximum lifetime benefit period has expired or the maximum lifetime amount has been paid out.

The days which are counted toward the lifetime maximum benefit period must be days for which the insured has actually received a benefit.

BENEFIT STANDARDS: Skilled nursing care, intermediate nursing care, home health care and adult day care benefits may be conditioned on the standard of "medically necessary" or "disability." Custodial care benefits may only be conditioned on the standard of "disability." Disability means needing assistance with at least 3 Activities of Daily Living (ADLs). ADLs to be used are: eating, toileting, mobility, bathing, dressing and continence.

ALZHEIMER'S DISEASE: Alzheimer's disease or other organically based dementia must be covered if diagnosed after the policy is purchased. Insurers must have established criteria other than brain biopsy or autopsy for determining the existence of a demonstrable organic cause.

ALCOHOLISM AND SUBSTANCE ABUSE: Coverage must be provided for any physical condition that is caused or complicated by alcoholism or substance abuse. Other treatment for alcoholism or substance abuse, i.e., alcohol or drug detoxification or rehabilitation, may be excluded.

PRE-EXISTING CONDITION: Unless the condition is specifically excluded, an illness that exists 6 months before the policy is purchased will be covered only after the policy is owned for 6 months.

GUARANTEED RENEWABLE: Policies must be at least guaranteed renewable. Policies shall continue and may not be cancelled for anything other than nonpayment of premium. Premiums may be increased but only for a whole class of people.

DISCLOSURE: Policies will have a required disclosure statement which will attempt to help consumers to better understand what benefits they are buying and what limitations and exclusions their policy has. All inflation rider offerings, whether at initial application or at any later date, must provide a separate inflation rider disclosure statement.

FLEXIBILITY: Companies may request that the Commissioner of Insurance modify a specific provision of the regulation. The Division of Insurance recognizes that long-term care insurance is still developing and that there needs to be some flexibility in regulating this type of insurance.

INFLATION RIDER: Companies must make an inflation rider available at the time of application (with no additional underwriting) to be purchased at the option of the policyholder.

NEGOTIATING WITH A NURSING HOME

For many people, the single most difficult decision they ever make is to put a parent or spouse into a nursing home. The decision always feels wrong. When the choice becomes unavoidable, it is made with guilt, sadness, and a sense of failure.

At such a time, you are emotionally unprepared to negotiate with a nursing home. Rather than shopping around to find the fairest price and researching the best services, the most you may be able to handle is one simple question: "Do you have a bed for my father?"

It's difficult enough to cope with the illness, let alone to investigate nursing homes. This chapter can't make the decision any less painful for you but it can help you understand how nursing homes operate and give you some tools to help you plan.

The Nursing Home's Agenda

You are in a better position to evaluate nursing homes if you understand something about how their finances operate. Nursing homes generally are paid by three sources: cash, Medicaid and nursing home insurance. By far, the two most common forms of payment are cash and Medicaid. In most states, well over 70% of the nursing home population is on Medicaid.

With few exceptions, the rate for private pay patients is much higher than Medicaid's rate — as much as twice as high. Nursing homes are reimbursed by Medicaid through a complex formula based on several factors, such as the age of the facility, level of care, location, and capital improvements. Medicaid builds a small profit into the rate it pays nursing homes. Their real profits come from those who pay privately.

Though the demand for beds exceeds the supply, nursing homes are not making the killing that many people think they are. Their costs for labor are high, especially in urban areas. Capital improvements to bring the facilities up to code are expensive. Any unanticipated problems, such as a delay in Medicaid reimbursement, can make the difference between survival and bankruptcy.

That's why there has been a major shake-out in the nursing home industry in recent years. Small independent operators, usually undercapitalized, have been forced to sell out to the large national chains. But even the large corporations find it difficult to make a go of it, especially in states which, because of their own money problems, do not reimburse promptly.

A perfect example is Massachusetts. In 1989, the legislature was forced to raise the income tax rate 15 percent to pay off an estimated $800 million in back Medicaid costs. Some bills to nursing homes were outstanding for as long as eight years!

Because of financial pressures, nursing homes try to avoid taking Medicaid applicants. The problem is so acute that every state and the federal government has a book full of rules prohibiting discrimination against Medicaid applicants .

Nevertheless, discrimination does occur every day.

The last thing you want to do is to make a speech to a nursing home about how it's illegal to discriminate against your parent or spouse. You do want to approach the nursing home from a position of strength. Strength means money.

Your Agenda

The rest of this chapter is useless to you unless you understand that you have to spend money to secure a bed in a good nursing home, even money that could be protected by following the steps we have covered in this book. In the real world, you have to buy your way into a nursing home. Average cost of the ticket: six to nine months private pay.

Here's how to find and get a bed in a good nursing home:

At least three to four months before an anticipated nursing home placement, begin researching your options. The factors to consider when evaluating a facility are: location, level of care provided, quality and cost.

Location

No decision about location should be made until all members of the family have been consulted. Which relatives will be visiting most often? Is there access to transportation? How close are other medical facilities such as hospitals?

Level of Care Provided

The ill person should be evaluated by the appropriate state or local authorities to determine the level of care required. Usually, the higher the level number, the less care necessary. A level III patient is generally able to look after himself with moderate assistance. A level II patient is generally bedridden and in need of constant custodial care. A level I patient requires continuing medical attention.

If the patient is going in on a private-pay basis at a more independent level of care (such as level III), make absolutely certain that the facility also takes at least level II patients. Some nursing homes, upon finding out that there are no more private funds, suddenly reclassify patients. If the facility does not provide the level of care needed, they can legitimately dump the patient.

Even though this may be wrong, the last thing you want is to get into an argument.

Quality of Care

The best way to find a good nursing home is to check with your local Council on Aging, state department of elderly affairs (if any), private groups such as Alzheimer's and Parkinson's support organizations, or a hospital social worker.

Costs

You should be the one to interview the nursing home about money, not the other way around. Find out what the costs are and the price of extras such as laundry, doctors' visits, and medications. Make sure that the facility is Medicaid certified. Find out what the policy is on when payment is due. Most states do not allow a nursing home to ask for a lump sum up front. If the subject comes up, don't make a speech about it, just suggest that the state may not allow it. (The objective is to find a bed for a person who desperately needs care, not start a lawsuit.)

Keep in mind that the nursing home wants to be sure there are private funds available. Therefore, you almost never get an answer to your question about bed availability until the nursing home gets an answer about who will pay. A commitment for a certain number of months of private pay is usually necessary to secure a bed.

10

LEGAL INSTRUMENTS

This chapter shows you how assets can be handled if you know that at some time in the future you will not be able to manage your own financial affairs. It is also for people who are making arrangements for friends or relatives who cannot presently handle their financial affairs.

Power of Attorney — Regular and Durable

A power of attorney is a legal instrument that gives to another or others the right to handle financial affairs. Typically, a person will create a power of attorney to give another the right to have access to a bank account or to sell stock on his behalf. The person given this responsibility does not have to be an attorney.

A **regular power of attorney** usually gives specific and limited powers like the ones mentioned above. It usually does not have an expiration date but ceases the minute you become incapacitated.

A **durable power of attorney** is exactly the same except that it remains valid even if you become incapacitated. It can be very effective in planning to protect assets which otherwise would have to be spent on a nursing home

Example: Peter is a widower with two children. He has $50,000 in cash and $10,000 in stock in his name only. His wife recently died in a nursing home. He is concerned about protecting his assets if he needs long-term care but does not want to give up control while he is still healthy.

Peter could simply put his children's names on his assets. However, if one of his children got divorced or got into financial trouble, his assets could be in jeopardy.

Or he could make up a durable power of attorney giving authority to one or both offspring to get at his assets should he become incapacitated. If he became ill and couldn't get at his assets, let alone manage them, his children could use the power of attorney to close out the accounts and transfer the assets to their names.

Warning: Giving a power of attorney is giving away control. It is not advisable to do this unless absolutely necessary. It is best to give it to someone who is trustworthy to hold *until it is needed*. Instructions should be given about how and when it will be used.

If your state allows it, consider putting two people on the power of attorney so there are checks and balances.

Consider a "springing" durable power of attorney. This instrument is valid only when you become incapacitated, unlike a regular or durable power of attorney which becomes effective the moment you sign.

Make sure you update! The biggest mistake lawyers and financial advisors make when recommending powers of attorney is to forget to inform their clients that most financial institutions will not accept them after a period of time. There is no set policy on when the instrument becomes "stale." Remember, a power of attorney is only as good as a person's or institution's willingness to accept it. Update by rewriting it (if only by changing the effective date) at least every two years.

Conservatorships

A conservatorship usually means that a person has requested of an appropriate court permission to handle the assets and affairs of someone who is incapacitated (the ward). Anyone can be named a conservator. In some states the ward can participate in choosing a conservator.

Once a person is appointed by the court, she becomes responsible for handling the assets in approximately the same way the ward would. Conservatorships are almost useless in protecting assets unless the ward has at least 30 months to plan to protect countable assets.

A durable power of attorney would be just as effective as a conservatorship at a fraction of the cost and without having the court and the world know your business.

Conservatorships are most effective when a person becomes so ill that long-term management of his/her assets is necessary. Readers of this book who have acted on what they learned should not find this alternative attractive or necessary.

Those with relatives who are already ill and who may need a nursing home down the road may think that a conservatorship is the answer. The problem is that Medicaid planning in practice means taking the assets out of the ward's name. A conservatorship, by definition, means keeping the assets in the ward's name but under the legal control of the conservator. Therefore, a conservator never gets assets away from Medicaid, but rather *preserves them* for Medicaid

Conservatorships therefore should not be considered unless you consult with an attorney who understands Medicaid.

Guardianships

A guardianship is the same as a conservatorship except that the court grants to the guardian control of the ward's body as well as his assets. The guardian requests that the court grant power to make decisions about such things as medication, treatment, and even matters of life and death.

On the subject of protecting assets, it is enough to say that a guardianship has the same advantages (not many) and disadvantages (many) as a conservatorship.

11

CHOOSING A LAWYER

Where to Look for a Lawyer

The practice of Medicaid law is a very specialized field. Few lawyers can speak its language fluently.

Here are some suggestions for finding an attorney with expertise in this field.

• Contact the National Academy of Elder Law Attorneys at 655 N. Alvernon Way, Suite 108, Tucson, Arizona 85711. This organization is made up of lawyers who specialize in problems of the elderly.

• Call your local council on aging or its equivalent for referrals.

• Speak to the social worker at your area hospital. Many have dealt with nursing home placement and are familiar with attorneys who work in the field.

• Speak to your doctor but make sure he has worked on *Medicaid* issues with the attorney he recommends.

• An excellent source of experienced attorneys is local support groups like Alzheimer's, Parkinson's and stroke victims' organizations.

• If you have a family lawyer whom you trust, ask him to find a lawyer who concentrates in the elder law field.

Here are some suggestions on how not to find an attorney.

• Don't choose an attorney from an advertisement. Anyone can call himself an expert.
• Don't rely on your local bar association referral service. Few if any have a category that deals with this subject. If they deal with it at all, they lump the subject with estate planning. Estate planners do not necessarily understand Medicaid.

Interviewing a Lawyer

Here are some points to raise with the attorney you are considering.

• What percentage of his practice is devoted to Medicaid law?
• Have him show you the specific regulations that cover Medicaid eligibility in your state. You'd be surprised how many lawyers don't have them.
• Ask if he has spoken or written on the subject.
• Ask him how he charges and specifically what work is performed. Make sure the attorney is willing to write you a comprehensive follow-up letter after your initial meeting. It is difficult to absorb everything the lawyer says in a first meeting. The letter will clarify questions raised and will give you the maximum benefit from this book.

After you have read this book, you will have identified the difficult points which a lawyer can help resolve. Mark the book and take it with you. Stop and listen to what he has to say about your problem. Does it seem that it's the first time he's heard it? Do you get the feeling you are giving more information to him than he to you? Does he repeatedly say to you "Let me look that up" or "I'll get back to you"? If the answer is yes to any of these, politely excuse yourself and find someone who speaks fluently.

THE CHARTS

Chart 1

This chart shows the minimum amount of countable assets each state allows the stay-at-home spouse to keep. Federal law permits each state to set a figure anywhere between a minimum of $12,000 and a maximum of $60,000, which goes up yearly.

Community Spouse Resource Allowance Minimum (MCCA 88)

AL	$12,000	KY	$60,000	ND	$60,000
AK	$60,000	LA	$12,000	OH	$12,000
AZ	$12,000	ME	$12,000	OK	$25,000
AR	$12,000	MD	$12,000	OR	$12,000
CA	$60,000	MA	$12,000	PA	$12,000
CO	$60,000	MI	$12,000	RI	$60,000
CT	$12,000	MN	$12,000	SC	$60,000
DE	$12,000	MS	$60,000	SD	$20,000
DC	N/R	MO	$12,000	TN	$12,000
FL	$60,000	MT	$12,000	TX	$12,000
GA	$60,000	NE	$12,000	UT	$12,000
HI	$60,000	NV	$12,000	VT	$60,000
ID	$12,000	NH	$12,000	VA	$12,000
IL	$60,000	NJ	$12,000	WA	$60,000
IN	$12,000	NM	$30,000	WV	$12,000
IA	$12,000	NY	$60,000	WI	$60,000
KS	$12,500	NC	$12,000	WY	$12,000

Key: N/R = No Response
SOURCE: NATIONAL GOVERNORS' ASSOCIATION, SEPTEMBER 1989

Chart 2

The states in this chart allow a single person to qualify for Medicaid benefits regardless of his monthly income, as long as it is less than the monthly nursing home bill.

States with No Limit on Income for Older Individuals Seeking Medicaid Coverage for Nursing-Home Costs

California	Nebraska
Connecticut	New Hampshire
District of Columbia	New York
Hawaii	North Carolina
Illinois	North Dakota
Indiana	Ohio
Kansas	Oregon
Kentucky	Pennsylvania
Maine	Rhode Island
Maryland	Utah
Massachusetts	Vermont
Michigan	Virginia
Minnesota	Washington
Missouri	West Virginia
Montana	Wisconsin

SOURCE: Edward Neuschler, *Medical Eligibility for the Elderly in Need of Long Term Care* (Report Prepared under Contract for the Congressional Research Service). Washington, D.C.: National Governors' Association Center for Policy Research (hereafter National Governors' Association Report"). Tables from the National Governors' Association Report generally reflect the most recent information effective as of July 1, 1987. Although most of the information remains accurate today, readers are advised to check with their state for exact information.

Chart 3

The states in this chart have set a limit of $1,062 on the amount of monthly income a single person can get and still qualify for Medicaid. If income is over this amount, benefits will be denied.

States with a $1,062 Limit* on Monthly Income for Older Americans Seeking Medicaid Coverage for Nursing-Home Bills

Alaska	New Jersey
Arkansas	Oklahoma
Colorado	South Carolina
Florida	South Dakota
Idaho	Tennessee
Iowa	Wyoming
Lousiana	

* The $1,062 income limit refers to total income from all sources before any deductions for 1988; the 1989 figure was not available at this writing but will be slightly higher.

SOURCE: National Governors' Association Report

The states in this chart have set a limit below $1,062 on the amount of monthly income a single person can get and still qualify for Medicaid. If income is over this amount, benefits will be denied.

States with Monthly Income Limits* Below $1,062 for Older Americans Seeking Medicaid Coverage for Nursing-Home Bills

State	Income Limit
Alabama	$852.90
Delaware	632.00
Georgia	937.00 (Net)
Nevada	734.00
New Mexico	871.00
Texas	658.65

* The $1,062 income limits refer to total income from all sources before any deductions, unless otherwise indicated. Net income refers to income after application of any disregards and deductions applied to determine Medicaid eligibility (normally the first $20 of unearned income is disregarded). In Florida and Georgia, in addition to the net income limit, gross income cannot exceed $1,062.
SOURCE: National Governors' Association Report

Chart 4

This chart applies to the nursing home resident only and tells how much of his monthly income can be put aside for his personal needs.

Personal-Needs Allowance Protected Out of Individual Income

State	Amount	State	Amount
Alabama	$30	Montana	$40
Alaska	70	Nebraska	30
Arkansas	30	Nevada	35
California	35	New Hampshire	35
Colorado	30	New Jersey	35
Connecticut	40	New Mexico	30
Delaware	31	New York	40
District of Columbia	60	North Carolina	30
Florida	30	North Dakota	45
Georgia	30	Ohio	30
Hawaii	30	Oklahoma	30
Idaho	30	Oregon	30
Illinois	30	Pennsylvania	30
Indiana	30	Rhode Island	30
Iowa	30	South Carolina	30
Kansas	30	South Dakota	30
Kentucky	40	Tennessee	30
Louisiana	33	Texas	30
Maine	35	Utah	30
Maryland	40	Vermont	40
Massachusetts	65	Virginia	30
Michigan	32	Washington	36.62
Minnesota	40	West Virginia	30
Mississippi	44	Wisconsin	40
Missouri	30	Wyoming	30

SOURCE: National Governors' Association Report.

Chart 5

This chart tells you what states allow a single person to maintain his home if it is likely that he will come home within a reasonable period of time (usually three to six months).

This allowance is usually available only if that person presents medical evidence of his ability to return. If your state is not on this chart, it means there is no allowance.

States Providing a Home-Maintenance Allowance

STATE	AMOUNT*	FLAT OR MAXIMUM** AMOUNT	MAXIMUM NO. OF MONTHS AVAILABLE
Alaska	$632	Flat	6
California	192	Flat	6
Colorado	185	Flat	6
Connecticut	Varies	Maximum	3
Delaware	75	Flat	None
District of Columbia	391	Flat	None
Idaho	212	Flat	6
Illinois	Varies	Maximum	6
Maryland	334	Flat	6
Massachusetts	455	Maximum	6
Minnesota	402	Maximum	3
Montana	340	Flat	6
Nebraska	140	Flat	6
New Hampshire	141	Flat	3
New Jersey	150	Maximum	6
New York	417	Flat	6 Subject to Extension
North Carolina	242	Flat	6
North Dakota	345	Flat	6
Oregon	Varies	None	None
Pennsylvania	372.40	Flat	6
Rhode Island	491.67	Maximum	6
South Carolina	340	Flat	6
Utah	262	Flat	6
Vermont	299	Flat	6
Virginia	Varies	Maximum	6
Washington	180	Flat	6
West Virginia	175	Flat	None
Wisconsin	442.72	Flat	6
Wyoming	150	Flat	6

* In the second column, "Varies" indicates that a home-maintenance allowance is provided, but that the amounts vary according to a state formula.
** In the third column, "Flat" indicates that this amount in all cases is the home-maintenance allowance; "Maximum" indicates the most that will be permitted under a formula adopted by the state.   SOURCE: National Governors' Association Report.

Chart 6

Amount of Cash a Person Can Protect from a Nursing Home

State	Amount	State	Amount
Alabama	$2,000	Montana	$2,000
Alaska	2,000	Nebraska	1,600
Arkansas	2,000	Nevada	2,000
California	2,000	New Hampshire	2,500
Colorado	2,000	New Jersey	2,000
Connecticut	1,600	New Mexico	2,000
Delaware	2,000	New York	3,000
District of Columbia	2,600	North Carolina	1,500
Florida	2,000	North Dakota	3,000
Georgia	2,000	Ohio	1,500
Hawaii	2,000	Oklahoma	2,000
Idaho	2,000	Oregon	2,000
Illinois	2,000	Pennsylvania	2,400
Indiana	1,500	Rhode Island	4,000
Iowa	2,000	South Carolina	2,000
Kansas	2,000	South Dakota	2,000
Kentucky	2,000	Tennessee	2,000
Louisiana	2,000	Texas	2,000
Maine	2,000	Utah	2,000
Maryland	2,500	Vermont	2,000
Massachusetts	2,000	Virginia	2,000
Michigan	2,000	Washington	2,000
Minnesota	3,750	West Virginia	2,000
Mississippi	2,000	Wisconsin	2,000
Missouri	999.99	Wyoming	2,000

SOURCE: National Governors' Association Report

Chart 7

The states are reimbursed 50% of their Medicaid expenses by the federal government. The government has its own regulations for Medicaid eligibility which they recommend that the states adopt but do not make mandatory.

One such regulation deals with re-classifying a person's house (primary residence) from a non-countable to a countable asset. The federal government says that if a single person is in a nursing home for more than a certain period of time the state has a right to terminate its' non-countable status and force the sale of the property to pay for the nursing home. This chart shows you which states have adopted this option.

Rules for Protecting a Person's House from a Nursing Home (a)

You will Be Protected:	If You Intend to Return (b)	If Your Doctor Certifies That You Are Likely to Recover Enough to Return	Whether or Not You Return	Any Time Limit on Protection?
Alabama (c)	X			NO
Alaska	X	X		NO
Arkansas	X			NO
California	X			NO
Colorado	X			NO
Connecticut (c)		X		9 mos.
Delaware	X			NO
District of Columbia	X			NO
Florida	X			NO
Georgia	X			NO
Hawaii	X			NO
Idaho	X			NO
Illinois	X			NO
Indiana (d)	X			NO

You will Be Protected:	If You Intend to Return	If Your Doctor Certifies That You Are Likely to Recover Enough to Return	Whether or Not You Return	Any Time Limit on Protection?
Iowa	X			NO
Kansas (e)	X	X		NO
Kentucky			X	NO
Louisiana	X			NO
Maine	X			NO
Maryland (c)	X	X		NO
Massachusetts			X	NO
Michigan			X	NO
Minnesota			X	6 mos.
Mississippi	X			NO
Missouri			X	NO
Montana		X		6 mos.
Nebraska		X		6 mos.
Nevada		X		NO
New Hampshire (e)		X		NO
New Jersey		X		6 mos.
New Mexico	X	X		NO
New York		X		NO
North Carolina		X		6 mos.
North Dakota		X	X	6 mos.
Ohio				6 mos.
Oklahoma	X	X		12 mos.
Oregon		X		6 mos.
Pennsylvania	X			NO
Rhode Island	X			NO

You will Be Protected:	If You Intend to Return	If Your Doctor Certifies That You Are Likely to Recover Enough to Return	Whether or Not You Return	Any Time Limit on Protection?
South Carolina	X			NO
South Dakota	X	X		6 mos.
Tennessee	X			NO
Texas	X			NO
Utah	X			NO
Vermont	X			NO
Virginia		X		6 mos.
Washington	X			NO
West Virginia	X			NO
Wisconsin		X		6 mos.
Wyoming	X			NO

(a) This table assumes that the older person has no spouse or dependent relative at home. If he or she does, the house in protected.

(b) The statement that you intend to return home must usually be made in writing.

(c) States have been permitted to adopt lien laws, allowing them to place liens of the homes of nursing-home residents receiving Medicaid. Liens may not be placed on a homer if living there is a nursing-home spouse, dependent children, or sibling who has an ownership interest in the home and has been living there for a year A nursing-home resident can probably block the imposition of a lien just by stating in writing his or her intent to return home. In any event, only three states, Alabama, Connecticut and Maryland have adopted lien laws to date.

(d) For residents of Indiana, one's home will be protected until either one has no intent to return or one is physically unable to return.

(e) For residents of Kansas, a home will be protected for three months without regard to whether the person will return; for residents of New Hampshire, a home will be protected for six months without regard to whether the person will return.

(f) For residents of Missouri, the state has a $23,000 limit on total assets, including the equity in one's house, until October 1, 1989. So if a person owens a home worth more than $23,000 (or less with other assets), he or she will have to sell the home and turn at least part of the proceeds over to the nursing home. After,October 1, 1989, one's home becomes a completely protected asset regardless of its value.   SOURCE: National Governors' Association Report

Chart 8

The primary non-countable asset, a person's home, is covered in Chart 7. Chart 8 deals with various other assets that states allow a Medicaid applicant to keep. If your state is not listed, it is because it did not respond to the National Governors' Association survey, which compiled this chart. In that case, take this chart to your department of public welfare and ask for their list of non-countable assets.

Assets Excluded from Medicaid Asset Eligibility Limits
(Other Than Home)

STATE	HOUSEHOLD GOODS	RINGS	CAR	INCOME-PRODUCING PROPERTY	OTHER PROPERTY FOR SUPPORT	LIFE INSURANCE	BURIAL COSTS
Connecticut	Up to $2,000	1 wedding, 1 engagement	1 up to $4,500	No equity limit	No limit	Excluded if face value below $1,500	Excluded up to $1,100
Hawaii	No jewelry except rings; all other household goods, no limit on value	1 wedding, 1 engagement	1 up to $1,500				Excluded up to $1,500
Illinois	Up to $2,000	1 wedding, 1 engagement	All vehicles fully exempt unless primarily for recreation	No equity limit	No limit	Excluded if face value below $1,500	Excluded up to $1,500
Indiana	No limit	1 wedding, 1 engagement	1 up to $4,500	Excluded up to $6,000, if property produces 6% return on excluded equity	Real property excluded only if producing food for home consumption	Excluded if face value below $1,400 and policy beneficiary is recipient's estate or funeral director	Excluded only if irrevocable
Minnesota	No limit	1 wedding, 1 engagement	1 up to $500	Excluded up to $6,000, if property produces 6% return on excluded equity	Not excluded unless not salable	Excluded if face value below $1,500	Excluded up to $1,500
Missouri	No limit	1 wedding, 1 engagement	1 vehicle without limit on value	No equity limit if used in trade or business		Excluded if face value below $1,500	Excluded only if irrevocable

Assets Excluded from Medicaid Asset Eligibility Limits (Other Than Home) (cont.)

STATE	HOUSEHOLD GOODS	RINGS	CAR	INCOME-PRODUCING PROPERTY	OTHER PROPERTY FOR SUPPORT	LIFE INSURANCE	BURIAL COSTS
Nebraska	Household goods of "moderate value"	1 wedding, 1 engagement	1 up to $1,500			Excluded if face value below $1,500	Excluded only if irrevocable
New Hampshire	No limit	1 wedding, 1 engagement	All vehicles fully exempt	No equity limit, excluded as long as income exceeds expenses		Excluded if face value below $1,500	Excluded only if irrevocable of for persons who are medically needy*
North Carolina	No limit	1 wedding, 1 engagement	1 up to $4,500	Excluded up to $6,000, if property produces 6% return on excluded equity		Excluded if face value below $1,500 — maximum for couple	Excluded up to $1,500
North Dakota	Up to $2,000	1 wedding, 1 engagement	1 up to $4,500	Excluded up to $6,000, if property produces 6% return on excluded equity	Equity up to $6,000 excluded	Excluded if face value below $1,500	Excluded up to $1,500
Ohio	No limit	1 wedding, 1 engagement	1 up to $4,500	Excluded up to $6,000, but if equity exceeds $6,000, entire equity is counted		Excluded if face value below $1,500	Excluded only if irrevocable

Assets Excluded from Medicaid Asset Eligibility Limits (Other Than Home) (cont.)

STATE	HOUSEHOLD GOODS	RINGS	CAR	INCOME-PRODUCING PROPERTY	OTHER PROPERTY FOR SUPPORT	LIFE INSURANCE	BURIAL COSTS
Oklahoma	No limit	1 wedding, 1 engagement	1 up to $4,500	Excluded up to $6,000, if property produces 6% return on excluded equity	Equity up to $6,000 excluded	Excluded if face value below $1,500	Excluded up to $1,500
Utah	Up to $2,000	1 wedding, 1 engagement	1 up to $4,500	Excluded up to $6,000, if property produces 6% return on excluded equity	Equity up to $6,000 excluded	Excluded if face value below $1,500	Excluded up to $1,500
Virginia	No limit	1 wedding, 1 engagement	1 vehicle without regard to purpose or value	Excluded up to $6,000, if property produces 6% return on excluded equity	Generally not excluded unless not salable	Excluded if face value below $1,500	Excluded only if irrevocalbe

SOURCE: National Governors' Association Report

* The medically needy are those people who do not receive cash assistance (Supplemental Security Income or state supplement) but who have limited income and resources and need help paying their bills.

NOTE: Burial plots are excluded.

Chart 9

State Medicaid Offices

ALABAMA
Dept. of Human
  Resources
64 N. Union St.
Montgomery, AL 36130
(205) 261-3190

ALASKA
Div. of Public Assistance
Health & Social Services
  Dept.
P.O. Box H
Juneau, AK 99811
(907) 465-3347

ARIZONA
Dept. of Economic
  Security
1717 W. Jefferson
Phoenix, AZ 85007
(602) 255-5678

ARKANSAS
Dept. of Human Services
1300 Donaghey Bldg.
Seventh & Main St.
Little Rock, AR 72201
(501) 371-1001

CALIFORNIA
Dept. of Social Services
744 P St.
Sacramento, CA 95814
(916) 445-2077

COLORADO
Dept. of Social Services
717 17th St.
Denver, CO 80202
(303) 294-5800

CONNECTICUT
Dept. of Income
  Maintenance
110 Bartholomew Ave.
Hartford, CT 06106
(203) 566-2008

DELAWARE
Div. of Economic Services
Health & Social Services
  Dept.
P.O. Box 906
New Castle, DE 19720
(302) 421-6734

FLORIDA
Economic Services
Health & Rehabilitative
  Services
1311 Winewood Blvd.
Tallahassee, FL 32301
(904) 488-3271

GEORGIA
Family & Children
  Services
Dept. of Human
  Resources
878 Peachtree St., NE
Atlanta, GA, 30309
(404) 894-6386

HAWAII
Public Welfare Div.
Dept. of Human Services
1390 Miller St.
Honolulu, HI 96813
(808) 548-5908

IDAHO
Div. of Welfare
Dept. of Health & Welfare
450 W. State St.
Boise, ID 83720
(208) 334-5747

ILLINOIS
Dept. of Public Aid
316 3. Second St.
Springfield, IL 62762
(217) 782-6716

INDIANA
Dept. of Public Welfare
100 N. Senate Ave.,
  Rm. 701
Indianapolis, IN 46204
(317) 232-4705

IOWA
Bur. of Economic
  Assistance
Dept. of Human Services
Hoover State Off. Bldg.
Des Moines, IA 50319
(515) 281-8629

KANSAS
Income Maintenance
Dept. of Social &
  Rehabilitative Services
6th Fl., State Off. Bldg.
Topeka, KS 66612
(913) 296-3271

KENTUCKY
Dept. for Social Insurance
Cabinet for Human
  Resources
275 E. Main St.
Frankfort, KY 40601
(502) 564-3703

LOUISIANA
Off. of Family Security
Health & Human
  Resources Dept.
P.O. Box 3776
Baton Rouge, LA 70821
(504) 342-3947

MAINE
Bur. of Income
  Maintenance
Dept. of Human Services
State House Station #11
Augusta, ME 04333
(207) 289-2415

MARYLAND
Social Services Admn.
Dept. of Human
  Resources
300 W. Preston St.
Baltimore, MD 21201
(301) 263-5200

MASSACHUSETTS
Dept. of Public Welfare
180 Tremont St.
Boston, MA 02111
(617) 727-6190

MICHIGAN
Dept. of Social Services
300 S. Capitol Ave.
P.O. Box 30037
Lansing, MI 48909
(517) 373-3500

MINNESOTA
Assistance Payments,
  Policy & Operations Div.
444 Lafayette Rd.
St. Paul, MN 55101
(612) 296-6955

MISSISSIPPI
Dept. of Public Welfare
515 E. Amite St.
P.O. Box 352
Jackson, MS 39205
(601) 354-0341

MISSOURI
Div. of Family Services
Dept. of Social Services
Broadway Bldg., Box 88
Jefferson City, MO 65103
(314) 751-4247

Chart 9

MONTANA
Dept. of Social &
  Rehabilitation Services
111 Sanders St.
Helena, MT 59601
(406) 444-5622

NEBRASKA
Dept. of Social Services
301 Centennial Mall S.
P.O. Box 95026
Lincoln, NE 68509
(402) 471-3121

NEVADA
Div. of Welfare
Dept. of Human
  Resources
2527 N. Carfion St.
Carson City, NV 89710

NEW HAMPSHIRE
Div. of Welfare
Dept. of Health &
  Welfare
Hazen Dr.
Concord, NH 03301
(603) 271-4321

NEW JERSEY
Div. of Public Welfare
Dept. of Human Services
6 Quakerbridge Plaza
Trenton, NJ 08625
(609) 588-2401

NEW MEXICO
Financial Assistance
  Bur.
Dept. of Human Services
P.O. Box 2348
Santa Fe, NM 87503
(5O5) 827-4429

NEW YORK
Dept. of Social Services
40 N. Pearl St.
Albany, NY 12243
(518) 474-9475

NORTH CAROLINA
Dept. of Human
  Resources
325 N. Salisbury St.
Raleigh, NC 27611
(919) 733-4534

NORTH DAKOTA
Dept. of Human Services
Judicial Wing, State
  Capitol
Bismarck, ND 58505
(701) 224-2310

OHIO
Dept. of Human Services
30 E. Broad St., 32nd Fl.
Columbus, OH 43266
(614) 466-6282

OKLAHOMA
Dept. of Human Services
P.O. Box 25352
Oklahoma City, OK 73125
(405) 521-3646

OREGON
Adult & Family
  Services Div.
Dept. of Human Resources
417 Public Service Bldg.
Salem, OR 97310
(503) 378-3680

PENNSYLVANIA
Dept. of Public Welfare
333 Health & Welfare Bldg.
Harrisburg, PA 17120
(717) 787-2600

RHODE ISLAND
Social & Economic
  Services
Dept. of Social &
Rehabilitative Services
600 New London Ave.
Cranston, RI 02920
(401) 464-2371

SOUTH CAROLINA
Dept. of Social Services
1535 Confederate Ave. Ext.
N. Complex
Columbia, SC 29202
(803) 734-5760

SOUTH DAKOTA
Office of Program Mgt.
Dept. of Social Services
Kneip Bldg.
Pierre, SD 57501
(605) 773-3165

TENNESSEE
Dept. of Human Services
111 Seventh Ave. N.12th Fl.
Nashville, TN 37219
(615) 741-2341

TEXAS
Dept. of Human Services
P.O. Box 2960
Austin, TX 78769
(512) 450-3030

UTAH
Off. of Assistance
  Payments
Dept. of Social Services
120 N. 200 W., 3rd Fl.
Salt Lake City, UT
84103
(801) 538-3970

VERMONT
Dept. of Social Welfare
Agcy. of Human Services
103 S. Main St.
Waterbury, VT 05676
(802) 241-2853

VIRGINIA
Dept. of Social Services
8007 Discovery Dr.
Richmond, VA 23288
(804) 281-9236

WASHINGTON
Income Assistance
  Services
Dept. of Social & Health
  Services
M/S OB-31C
Twelfth & Franklin
Olympia, WA 98504
(206) 753-3080

WEST VIRGINIA
Dept. of Human Services
1900 Washington St. E.
Bldg. 6, Rm. 617-B
Charleston, WV 25305
(304) 348-2400

WISCONSIN
Div. of Community
  Services
Dept. of Health &
  Social Services
One W. Wilson St.
Box 7850
Madison, WI 53707
(608) 266-0554

WYOMING
Public Assistance and
  Social Services
Health & Social Services
  Dept.
Hathaway Bldg.
Cheyenne, WY 82002
(307) 777-7564

DISTRICT OF COLUMBIA
Income Maintenance
  Admn.
Dept. of Human Services
500 First St., NW
Rm. 9000
Washington, DC 20001
(202) 724-5506

Chart 9

NORTHERN MARIANA ISLANDS
Dept. of Community &
 Cultural Affairs
Off. of the Governor
Saipan, CM 96950
(670) 322-9722

PUERTO RICO
Dept. of Social Services
P.O. Box 11398
Santurce, PR 00910
(809) 722-7400

VIRGIN ISLANDS
Dept. of Human Services
Barbel Plaza S.
St. Thomas, VI 00802
(809) 774-0930

Chart 10

State Insurance Commission Addresses

ALABAMA
135 South Union Street #160
Montgomery, Alabama 36130-
3401
1-205-269-3550

ALASKA
P.O. Box 'D'
Juneau, Alaska 99811
1-907-465-2515

AMERICAN SAMOA
Office of the Governor
Pago Pago, American Samoa
96796
1-684-633-4116

ARIZONA
3030 No. 3rd St., Suite 1100
Phoenix, Arizona 85012
1-602-255-5400

ARKANSAS
400 University Tower Bldg.
12th & University Street
Little Rock, Arkansas 72204
1-501-371-1325

Members of the NAIC

CALIFORNIA
100 Van Ness Avenue
San Francisco, California 94102
1-415-557-9624

COLORADO
303 West Colfax Avenue
5th Floor
Denver, Colorado 80204
1-303-620-4300

CONNECTICUT
165 Capitol Avenue
State Office Building
Room 425
Hartford, Connecticut 06106
1-203-566-5275

DELAWARE
841 Silverlake Boulevard
Dover, Delaware 19901
1-302-736-4251

DISTRICT OF COLUMBIA
613 G. Street, NW
6th Floor
Washington, D.C. 20001
1-202-727-5422

FLORIDA
State Capitol
Plaza Level Eleven
Tallahassee, Florida 32399-0300
1-904-488-3440

GEORGIA
2 Martin L. King, Jr. Dr.
704 West Tower
Atlanta, Georgia 30334
1-404-656-2056

GUAM
P.O. Box 2796
Agana, Guam 96910
or
855 West Marine Drive
011-671-477-1040

HAWAII
P.O. Box 3614
Honolulu, Hawaii 96811
1-808-548-5450

IDAHO
500 South l0th Street
Boise, Idaho 83720
1-208-334-2250

Chart 10

ILLINOIS
320 West Washington St. 4th Flr.
Springfield, Illinois 62767
1-217-782-4515

INDIANA
311 West Washington Street
Suite 300
Indianapolis, Indiana 46204-2787
1-317-232-2386

IOWA
Lucas State Office Building
6th Floor
Des Moines, Iowa 50319
1-515-281-5705

KANSAS
420 S.W. 9th Street
Topeka, Kansas 66612
1-913-296-7801

KENTUCKY
229 West Main Street
P.O. Box 517
Frankfort, Kentucky 40602
1-501-564-3630

LOUISIANA
P.O. Box 94214
Baton Rouge, Louisiana 70804-
 9214
or 950 North 5th Street
Baton Rouge, Louisiana 70804-
 9214
1-504-342-5328

178

MAINE
State Office Building
State House, Station 34
Augusta, Maine 04333
1-207-582-8707

MARYLAND
501 St. Paul Place
(Stanbalt Bldg.)
7th Floor-South
Baltimore, Maryland 21202
1-301-333-2520

MASSACHUSETTS
280 Friend Street
Boston, Massachusetts 02114
1-617-727-7189

MICHIGAN
P.O. Box 30220
Lansing, Michigan 48909
or
611 West Ottawa Street
2nd Floor,
North Lansing, Michigan 48933
1-517-373-9273

MINNESOTA
500 Metro Square Building
5th Floor
St. Paul, Minnesota 55101
1-612-296-6848

MISSISSIPPI
1804 Walter Sillers Bldg.
P.O. Box 79
Jackson, Mississippi 39205
1-601-359-3569

MISSOURI
301 West High Street 6 North
P.O. Box 690
Jefferson City, Missouri 65102-
 0690
1-314-751-2451

MONTANA
126 North Sanders
Mitchell Building
Room 270
PO. Box 4009
Helena, Montana 59601
1-406-444-2040

NEBRASKA
Terminal Building
941 O Street, Suite 400
Lincoln, Nebraska 68508
1-402-471-2201

NEVADA
Nye Building
201 South Fall Street
Carson City, Nevada 89701
1-702-885-4270

NEW HAMPSHIRE
169 Manchester Street
Concord, New Hampshire 03301
1-603-271-2261

NEW JERSEY
20 West State Street CN325
Trenton, New Jersey 08625
1-609-292-5363

NEW MEXICO
Pera Bldg.
P.O. Drawer 1269
Santa Fe, New Mexico 87504-
1269
1-505-827-4500

NEW YORK
160 West Broadway
New York, New York 10013
1-212-602-0429

NORTH CAROLINA
Dobbs Bldg.
P.O. Box 26387
Raleigh, North Carolina 27611
1-919-733-7343

NORTH DAKOTA
Capitol Bldg.
Fifth Floor
Bismarck, North Dakota 58505
1-701-224-2440

OHIO
2100 Stella Court
Columbus, Ohio 43266-0566
1-614-644-2658

OKLAHOMA
P.O. Box 53408
Oklahoma City, Oklahoma
73152-3404
or 1901 North Walnut
Oklahoma City, Oklahoma 73105
1-405-521-2828

OREGON
21 Labor & Industries Bldg.
Salem, Oregon 97310
1-503-378-4271

PENNSYLVANIA
Strawberry Square
13th Floor
Harrisburg, Pennsylvania 17120
1-717-787-5173

PUERTO RICO
Fernandez Juncos Station
P.O. Box 8330
Santurce, PR 00910
I-809-722-8686

RHODE ISLAND
233 Richmond St., Suite 237
Providence, Rhode Island
02903-4237
I-401-277-2246

SOUTH CAROLINA
1612 Marion Street
Columbia, South Carolina 29201
or
P.O. Box 100105
Columbia, South Carolina 29202-
3105
1-803-737-6117

SOUTH DAKOTA
Insurance Building
910 E. Sioux Avenue
Pierre, South Dakota 57501
1-605-773-3563

TENNESSEE
Volunteer Plaza
500 James Robertson Pkwy.
Nashville, Tennessee 37219
1-615-741-2241

TEXAS
1110 San Jacinto Blvd.
Austin, Texas 78701-1998
1-512-463-9979

UTAH
P.O. Box 45803
Salt Lake City, Utah 84145
or
160 E. Third Street
Heber M. Wells Bldg.
Salt Lake City, Utah 84145
1-801-530-6400

Chart 10

VERMONT
State Office Building
Montpelier, Vermont 05602
1-802-828-3301

VIRGINIA
700 Jefferson Building
P.O. Box 1157
Richmond, Virginia 23209
1-804-786-3741

VIRGIN ISLANDS
Kongens Gade #18
St. Thomas, V.I. 00802
1-809-774-2991

WASHINGTON
Insurance Building AQ21
Olympia, Washington 98504
1-206-753-7301

WEST VIRGINIA
2019 Washington Street, E
Charleston, West Virignia 25305
1-304-348-3394

WISCONSIN
P.O. Box 7873
123 West Washington Ave.
Madison, Wisconsin 53702
1-608-266-0102

WYOMING
Herschler Building
122 West 25th Street
Cheyenne, Wyoming 82002
1-307-777-7401

INDEX